RING OF FIRE

RING OF FIRE

High-Stakes Mining in a
Lowlands Wilderness

Virginia Heffernan

Published by ECW Press
665 Gerrard Street East
Toronto, Ontario, Canada M4M 1Y2
416-694-3348 / info@ecwpress.com

Cover design: Michel Vrana

LIBRARY AND ARCHIVES CANADA CATALOGUING
IN PUBLICATION

Title: Ring of fire : high-stakes mining in a lowlands
wilderness / Virginia Heffernan.

Names: Heffernan, Virginia, author.

Description: Includes bibliographical references and
index.

Identifiers: Canadiana (print) 2022042957X
Canadiana (ebook) 20220429642

ISBN 978-1-77041-674-1 (softcover)
ISBN 978-1-77852-162-1 (ePub)
ISBN 978-1-77852-163-8 (PDF)
ISBN 978-1-77852-164-5 (Kindle)

Subjects: LCSH: Mineral industries—James Bay
Region. | LCSH: Mineral industries—Environmental
aspects—James Bay Region. | LCSH: Mineral
industries—Social aspects—James Bay Region. |
LCSH: Indigenous peoples—Civil rights—James Bay
Region.

Classification: LCC HD9506.C22 H44 2023 | DDC
338.209714/115—dc23

This book is funded in part by the Government of Canada. *Ce livre est financé en partie par le gouvernement du
Canada.* We also acknowledge the support of the Government of Ontario through the Ontario Book Publishing Tax
Credit, and through Ontario Creates.

PRINTED AND BOUND IN CANADA

PRINTING: FRIESENS   5 4 3 2 1

*To my father, Jerry (1919–), who encouraged
my study of geology as a portal to the world*

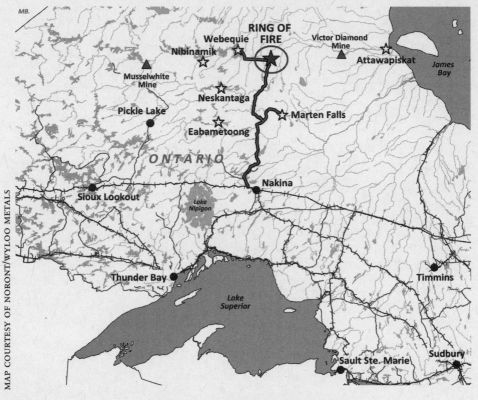

PROPOSED ROAD TO THE RING OF FIRE

The Ring of Fire is a 5,000-square-kilometre crescent of ancient volcanic rock rich in nickel, copper, and other metals considered critical to the global transition to renewable energy. The metal deposits lie hidden beneath the remote swamps of the Hudson Bay and James Bay Lowlands of northern Canada, the second-largest temperate wetland in the world. The area is home to several thousand Indigenous people in communities accessible only by plane or winter road. The deposits, too, are stranded by a lack of infrastructure. In 2022, Canada and the province of Ontario pledged billions of dollars towards a critical-minerals strategy, including building an all-weather road to the Ring of Fire.

CONTENTS

INTRODUCTION

Tremors of Disruption

S cott Jacob scans the sea of suits. He points to the only chairs remaining in the makeshift food court assembled to feed and water thousands. We scurry over to them, heads down, weaving through the crowd.

About 23,000 people — more than enough to fill a National Hockey League arena — are gathered deep in the bowels of the Metro Toronto Convention Centre on this day in early March 2020. They've flown in from more than 100 countries and remote Canadian communities to participate in the world's largest mining event, the Prospectors & Developers Association of Canada (PDAC) convention.

The four-day whirlwind of deal-making and partying, held annually, is timed to coincide with spring thaw, when prospectors traditionally emerged from the Canadian bush for a few weeks of leisure before heading back to their claim holdings. But the ninety-year-old event's renown as a hotspot of fundraising for mineral exploration and mine development has long since spread beyond Canada's borders.

This year, the Chinese delegation and its supersized marquee are noticeably absent. Hand sanitizer dispensers have replaced the usual swag at the exhibitor booths. But you would never know from all the handshaking and bear-hugging going on that the world is in the grips of the highly contagious COVID-19 virus. We'd soon find out what that carelessness cost.

The business of reunion going on around us sounds like a massive cocktail party. Indeed, until relatively recently in the convention's history, the men would have been enjoying free beers with their lunch, not four-dollar bottles of water. The rare woman walking the floor would more likely identify as a convention booth bunny than a geoscientist or financier. When I first started to attend the event as a member of the press in the 1990s, I was advised to leave my heels at home unless I wanted to be propositioned. Any Indigenous person brave enough to attend might well have been shown the door.

Passions run high when fortunes reach the level of risk that mineral exploration investments inherently involve. In those days, disagreements would occasionally evolve into brawls amid the all-day drinkers at the convention. Once, around the dinner hour, two old friends and business associates from northeastern Ontario had a falling-out. On March 9, 1987, Timmins "Timmy" Bissonnette gunned down stock promoter Guy Lamarche with a silver-plated revolver on the escalator of the Royal York, the grand old hotel that had been hosting the convention since 1944. Lamarche died on the scene. Bissonnette was sentenced to life in prison.

The convention's Wild West nature has since been replaced with a much more corporate vibe. Female representation in the sector has increased incrementally, to 16 percent in Canada. But the biggest change, with the introduction and growth of Indigenous programming this century, is the acknowledgement by industry and government that Indigenous peoples have a significant role to play as partners in exploration and mining.

✳

With a few sweeps of his forearm, Jacob — former chief of the Webequie First Nation, an Ojibway community in far northern Ontario — wipes the crumbs off the corner of the long table jammed with men wolfing down triangular sandwiches from clear plastic containers. He gestures for me to take a seat beside him on a stackable chair still radiating heat from its last occupant.

We have to shout to make ourselves heard over the din. Jacob is describing what it was like for him, as chief of the nearest community to the Ring of Fire, to be hit by a sudden surge of helicopters and prospectors descending on Webequie in the James Bay Lowlands in the summer of 2007, when the first nickel discovery was made. Prospectors ply their trade not only for the adventure of exploration and discovery, but for the slim chance a public company may come along one day, option their claims, and turn them into mines that pay royalties. At the time, Jacob wasn't sure whether to be pleased or angry about the rush, "but our elders told us, just be prepared for what is to come."

Jacob says the Webequie elders recalled what had happened to another Ojibway First Nation, Mishkeegogamang, to this day the most northerly Indigenous community in the province to have all-weather road access. When Ontario decided to build the road, Highway 599, north from Thunder Bay to service gold deposits in the area in the 1950s, the province relocated the Mishkeegogamang reserve closer to the highway. Community members had no say in either the road building or the relocation. Coinciding with a new system of social assistance from Ottawa, the move drastically changed their way of life, and most had to abandon hunting, fishing, and trapping.

"The people were not used to living together year-round in a large group, and there was too little full-time employment," according to Mishkeegogamang's website. "Traditional structures had broken down, and new organizations had not yet taken their place effectively."

A similar tragedy continues to play out decades later in many of the Indigenous communities under Treaty 9 (also known as the James Bay Treaty), covering present-day Ontario north of the land separating the Great Lakes watershed from the Hudson and James Bay drainage basins. Signed in 1905–06, after Confederation, the purpose of the treaty was to buy land and resources from Cree and Ojibway peoples to allow for white settlement and resource development. In exchange, the Indigenous residents were to receive cash payments, reserves to live on, education for their children, and hunting, fishing, and trapping rights. But the treaty turned out to be a lopsided deal deeply favouring the settlers.

As part of the settlement effort, Ontario passed the Mines Act of 1906, allowing prospectors to move freely through the wilderness armed with picks and shovels. Even today, anyone over the age of eighteen can obtain a prospector's licence granting entry to "Crown Land." About 87 percent of Ontario's land mass is considered by the federal and provincial governments to belong to the Crown.

Until recently, if a prospector found valuable minerals or even had a hunch they might exist, they could simply cut four lines through the bush, hammer in wooden claim posts at the four corners of the square, register the claim with the province, and take ownership of whatever valuable minerals lay within. They had an obligation to "work" the claim so it wouldn't lie fallow — mapping, rock sampling, and so forth — but otherwise were free to prospect. In 2012 the province revised what is now called the Ontario Mining Act to require Indigenous consultation before exploration takes place. And in 2018, the province moved to an online map-staking system. But the spirit of the law remains the same.

Treaty 9 overlaps with what is known as Ontario's Far North, an area twice the size of the United Kingdom, stretching from the Manitoba border in the west to James Bay in the east. The Far North contains the world's second-largest temperate wetland and largest boreal forest untouched by development. It is home to roughly 24,000 people (90 percent First Nations) in thirty-one communities. The Cree call it the Breathing Lands, the lungs of Canada. The area is so remote that some of its rivers remain unmapped.

The Ring of Fire — where the metal endowment includes not just nickel, copper, and platinum group metals but chromium, gold, and zinc — lies at the heart of this unique and special region. Naturally, the Ojibway, Cree, and Oji-Cree (a blend that occurred as Ojibway moved north into Cree territory during the fur trade) communities near and downstream of the Ring of Fire insist on playing a significant role in the decision-making around any proposed mining development as a way to minimize environmental damage and share in the resulting wealth.

The Constitution Act of 1982 enshrined Indigenous rights to be consulted by the Crown on activities that could adversely affect them, including mineral exploration and mining. Supreme Court rulings over the past two decades have affirmed this right. Though consultation does not imply a veto on development, "free, prior, and informed consent" — the wording of the United Nations Declaration on the Rights of Indigenous Peoples adopted by Canada in 2021 — perhaps does.

We're at a watershed moment in Canadian and global history, when Indigenous peoples are taking some control over resource development on their traditional lands.

*

As an exploration geoscientist turned mining journalist, I was naturally drawn to the fevered excitement of the 2007 Ring of Fire mineral discovery and its potential to become a major international source of several important metals. But my initial perspective was too narrow. As years passed and Indigenous communities across Canada exercised their constitutional right to be consulted on resource development, the fate of the remote region became increasingly uncertain, and the implications of the ongoing discoveries more intriguing. The mineral-rich area encapsulates all the challenges of resource development in Canada: the potential for environmental damage, a lack of infrastructure that leaves resources stranded, and a regulatory and Indigenous consultation process that can be opaque. Although the mining sector accounts for roughly 5 percent of the nation's GDP and employs about 700,000 people directly and indirectly (with mining workers earning an average annual salary of C$123,000 in 2019), these challenges threaten further investment.

By 2012, the Ring of Fire was shaping up to be an epic three-way battle among a mining industry unaccustomed to having its ownership of mineral discoveries questioned, a provincial government that considered Indigenous relations to be a federal matter, and members of First Nations communities who took their right to consultation seriously, along with their duty to protect the land for future generations. More than a decade later, recognition that the region's nickel, copper, and other metals could play a significant role in the world's transition to renewable energy added an extra layer of complexity. Did the contentious Ring of Fire stand a chance of ever being developed?

If not, the opportunity cost would be high. By virtue of its size, relative infancy in the exploration-mining sequence, and critical mineral endowment, the Ring of Fire represents an unprecedented chance to build a global model of resource management in which benefits to country and community far outweigh social and environmental costs. To allow the Ring of Fire to smoulder amid ongoing conflict would be irresponsible to all stakeholders.

Indigenous partnership will be the catalyst for development. The mineral exploration and mining sector is already the largest private-sector employer of Indigenous people and an important client for Indigenous-owned businesses in Canada. The Ring of Fire itself is one of the most significant metal discoveries of the twenty-first century and has the potential to become a long-lasting mining camp. Electric vehicle manufacturers, and other green revolution capitalists, are eager to get their hands on the area's critical metals and minerals. But a measured, collaborative approach to mining development in this fragile area that is more in line with Indigenous sensibilities is the only way to avoid perpetuating the inequities of the past.

✳

By our meeting at PDAC 2020, Jacob had become the manager of community relations for Noront Resources, the main industry player in the Ring of Fire; he tells me he would move back to his fly-in community of Webequie from his current home in Thunder Bay if there were any housing available. He still has older family members there and some of them are fragile. Most suffered from abuse at the residential school they were forced to attend. They struggle with their mental and/or physical health as a result. One uncle simply disappeared, never to return from boarding.

As we chat about personal tragedy amid the moneymaking melee, a Who's Who of Indigenous leaders either stops to talk or waves from a distance. There's David Paul Achneepineskum, CEO of the Matawa Tribal Council, which represents nine First Nations and 10,000 people in the region near the Ring of Fire. And here comes his cousin, Bruce Achneepineskum, chief of one of those Nations, Marten Falls, which lies about 100 kilometres southeast of the mineral deposits. Taking a seat across from us and sporting a leather cowboy hat is Jerry Asp, former chief of the powerful Tahltan Nation in B.C., founder of the largest Indigenous-owned heavy construction company in western Canada, and member of the Mining Hall of Fame. He devours a Styrofoam bowl of noodle soup as he reminisces about flying planeloads of Kentucky Fried Chicken into Webequie when he was advising the band council there on how to proceed with the Ring of Fire. Jacob erupts in laughter at the memory.

Next, fellow Hall of Famer Mackenzie "Mac" Watson sidles over to greet us. Watson is a geologist whose junior company, Freewest Resources, discovered the chromite that put the Ring of Fire on the world stage. He gives Jacob a ribbing about the dormant status of the development a decade after he sold Freewest to an American mining company for C$240 million in cash. "Get that road up there so you can get some work for the kids!" he exclaims over his shoulder as he drifts back into the crowd to the tune of Jacob's ringtone — you guessed it, Johnny Cash's "Ring of Fire."

Watson must be reading Jacob's mind because as we speak, Ontario premier Doug Ford and Greg Rickford, his minister of Energy, Northern Development, and Mines (and minister of Indigenous Affairs) are making their way to the Ontario pavilion. They are about to announce an agreement with the current chief of Webequie, Cornelius Wabasse, and Marten Falls' Achneepineskum to do just that. Dubbed the Northern Road Link, the new road would connect Marten Falls and Webequie to each other and to the provincial highway system for the first time.

Jacob is pumped about the announcement, saying it represents the most progress made for Indigenous communities in northern Ontario in years. But the road has yet to be embraced by some of the other seven Nations in the Matawa Tribal Council. Some are downright opposed to it. Following the press conference, the media spotlight swivels to Chief Chris Moonias of Neskantaga First Nation, a tiny community 130 kilometres upriver of the proposed mining camp. He is concerned about how the road and other developments will affect the Attawapiskat River watershed that begins at his community and runs through the Ring of Fire on its way to James Bay. "You can expect opposition if Ontario, or any road proponent, tries to put a shovel in the ground of our territory without our consent," he tells *CKDR News*.[1]

Later in the day, the cracks in the tribal council become even more apparent when only five of the nine chiefs attend a panel discussion on development of Ontario's Far North. Those who do participate say their priorities lie with housing and clean drinking water before development.

"There is opportunity in the air, but I think before we talk about billion-dollar projects in our region, we would like to have some of our infrastructure dealt with," Chief Harvey Yesno of Eabametoong First Nation tells the audience. "We've had 115 years of illegal seizure and occupation by Ontario. I think you can see the inequity in that land swindle."

It's the same message put forward in 2006 when the PDAC convention introduced Indigenous programming to foster more collaboration, namely to put First Nations, Inuit, and Métis on a level playing field with the rest of Canada's citizens so they have, at the very least, the capacity to deal with resource negotiations. The country and the province have spent tens of millions towards this goal in the James Bay Lowlands but have achieved next to nothing: Neskantaga is entering its twenty-sixth year of a boil-water advisory; a bag of milk costs C$15; gas is C$2.20 per litre; dwellings house up to eighteen people.

Outside the convention, a couple of hundred protesters have gathered on Toronto's Front Street yelling "Shame!" Some are in solidarity with the Wet'suwet'un hereditary chiefs, who are opposing the Coastal GasLink project in B.C.; others are protesting environmental and human rights abuses by Canadian miners overseas. The protesters would like to stop or curtail most resource extraction.

Today feels like a pivotal moment for Canadians and our resource-dependent economy. What will it take to move forward towards a common goal?

PART I

Prospectors and Promoters

CHAPTER I

Volcanoes, Glaciers, and Ancient Seas

In the unlikely event that you found yourself traipsing through the remote swamp harbouring the Ring of Fire, you'd never imagine that beneath your waterlogged boots was a trove of metal deposits to rival some of the richest in the world. Even if you were a trained geologist, there would be scant evidence to point to a potential mining camp because the rocks hosting the metals lie hidden beneath a thick cap of muskeg — an acidic peat anchoring scattered patches of moss and stunted trees — as well as sand, gravel, and, below that, limestone.

This cover-up is the handiwork of the last ice age, which began a little over 2.5 million years ago and ended 10,000 years back. During this period, ice sheets up to three kilometres thick blanketed almost all of Canada and most of the northern U.S., Europe, and Asia. The sheet centred on Hudson Bay and covering modern-day Ontario and Quebec was called Laurentide.

Laurentide was dynamic, expanding and contracting like a beating heart in response to brief warming and cooling periods. All that forceful movement over hundreds of thousands of years scraped and pulverized the rock below, re-depositing it as sand and gravel known as glacial till. At the same time, the weight of the ice pressed the land down like a human would a mattress.

But by about 8,000 years ago, the climate was warming quickly and irrevocably. Laurentide was on its last legs, already split in two and dripping water relentlessly from its edges and underbelly. The waters in

Hudson and James Bay expanded in response. They overflowed their western banks, rushing into the bowl of depressed land to form a water body later named the Tyrrell Sea (after the renowned Canadian geologist Joseph Tyrrell, who led several expeditions into Canada's north). The sea spread westward 100 to 250 kilometres. It is estimated to have been about 280 metres deep, nearly as deep as the Eiffel Tower is tall.

Then, not nearly as dramatically, the sea contracted as the last of the heavy ice sheet disappeared. Released from its burden, the land was free to rebound. Still sodden, underlain by permafrost, and poorly drained, the area that had been submerged for so long was now rising and ripe for the formation of muskeg: the top, and most recent, layer blanketing the Ring of Fire deposits of chromium, copper, gold, nickel, zinc, and other metals. The slow but dynamic rebound continues to this day, adding approximately two kilometres of shoreline per century.

Beneath this spongy swamp that makes infrastructure logistics challenging lies a thick layer (up to 300 metres in some areas) of limestone formed long before the last ice age on the floors of seas warm enough to swim in as they washed over the area repeatedly 350–450 million years ago. The beds of sedimentary rock accumulated as calcium carbonate crystallized in the warm water and carcasses of sea urchins and coral decomposed. Today, the gravel bars lining the rivers of the James Bay watershed are littered with evidence of these ancient sea creatures preserved in limestone pebbles, a budding paleontologist's paradise.

You'd have to dig a little deeper to find the rocks hosting the Ring of Fire mineral deposits. They are among the oldest and most stable in the world, dating back to when Earth was still a turbulent teenager nearly three billion years ago. The cracks that formed within them as the planet later groaned and shifted are the ideal conduits for hot magma rising up from Earth's mantle. But these so-called basement rocks rarely poke their heads above the thick cover of sand, gravel, and limestone in the James Bay Lowlands.

In the swamp, there's only one way to see this ancient metal-rich geology and its peculiarities without embarking on the expensive business of drilling: by employing geophysics to see through the cover layers. As far back as the 1960s, the Geological Survey of Canada was flying airborne surveys over the lowlands to detect magnetic variations in the rocks and constructing maps to interpret the hidden geology. But it wasn't until De Beers, the global diamond monopoly, found diamonds in the lowlands in the 1980s that geoscientists began to view these preliminary maps, and the ones that would follow, with an eye to mineral wealth.

Some in the academic world were indignant when the late Richard Nemis, the promoter responsible for kickstarting the mineral rush to the area, named his discovery the "Ring of Fire" after a song by Johnny Cash, his favourite performer. The Ring of Fire is formal nomenclature for a seismically active belt that encircles the Pacific Ocean. It seemed grandiose to give this swampy morass in northern Ontario the same name as such a globally significant geological feature. But Nemis was onto something bigger than fan love.

Geologists now speculate that the only way Nemis's ring could contain so much mantle-derived (or ultramafic) magma and metal was if some cataclysmic geological event, such as two continents colliding or separating, had cracked open the basement rocks.[1] Imagine a ship washing up on a shoal, floorboards splintering. When the ship returns to sea, the water rushes in. The same physics are at play when continents collide, one sliding over the other and shattering the surrounding rock with the force of the collision. When the landmass retreats, rifts open up, allowing magma to flow rapidly to surface. The modern-day analogues are the violent rumblings and eruptions along the official Ring of Fire in places such as Washington State, Japan, and the Philippines.

Now cast your mind back 2.7 billion years. The crust is splitting apart just west of the current imprint of Hudson Bay. The crust is thinner and the core hotter than now, creating a lot of melted mantle with nowhere to go. So as soon as a rift opens up, the restless magma lets loose and ascends. When the magma reaches a point of neutral buoyancy — the point where its density equals that of the surrounding rocks — it begins to spread horizontally along planes of weakness, such as the contacts between different rock types or faults in the bedrock. Then imagine this eruption reoccurring in several violent pulses over a relatively short geological span of a few million years.

On its way to surface, the intense heat of these magmas partially melts the surrounding rocks, introducing sulphur into the mix. The sulphur readily combines with iron, nickel, copper, and platinum group elements

(PGEs) in the magma to form distinct droplets. Like oil and water, the sulphide droplets refuse to mix with the surrounding liquid. Instead, they gather together into ever-larger droplets, becoming heavier and heavier and eventually sinking to the bottom of the magma chamber. As the magma flow slows, vertical cracks filled with liquid are frozen in time, forming feeder dikes richly concentrated in metals.

These concentrating factors make the metal grades of the "magmatic" Ring of Fire deposits high by international standards. The first one that would be mined, Eagle's Nest, has grades averaging 1.7 percent nickel and 1 percent copper, with significant quantities of palladium, the shiny silvery-white metal used in the catalytic converters of cars. By comparison, one of the world's largest undeveloped nickel sulphide deposits, the Dumont project in Quebec, has grades of about 0.27 percent nickel.[2] Eagle's Nest resembles a long skinny structure taller than two CN Towers but with a relatively tiny footprint at surface — hard to find but worth it when you do. There are dozens more nickel-copper-PGE targets just like Eagle's Nest in the Ring of Fire, and these long skinny dikes are just one part of a remarkable metal endowment deposited so long ago.

So cast your mind back again. Imagine the magma, while moving vertically, was also spreading in horizontal, tabular sheets called sills. Here's where the chromium crystallized and rained out in large volumes in separate but related deposits, which were given names such as Blackbird and Black Thor to reflect the dark colour and hardness of the massive chromite layers. This sill complex stretches for about 16 kilometres and is up to 1.5 kilometres thick. The thickness of the chromite layers within the sills is globally exceptional, up to 100 metres, about the height of Big Ben. The grades are some of the highest, up to 35–40 percent chromium-oxide. To say the chromite deposits in the Ring of Fire are world class is clichéd but understated.

Finally, at the top of the geological sequence, above the vertical nickel-copper feeder dikes and horizontal chromite-rich sills, lies a series of copper-zinc deposits known as volcanogenic massive sulphide (VMS) deposits. The VMS deposits formed when bubbling hot magma heated seawater that had seeped through cracks under the seafloor (recall the ancient seas that washed over the area), causing it to circulate and dissolve metals in its wake. Eventually this hot water erupted back onto the seafloor. The rapid cooling that ensued allowed the metals to form distinct lenses of high-grade copper-zinc mineralization. These VMS lenses tend to occur in clusters; explorers believe there are many more to be found in the Ring of Fire.

And although unsurprising, it was thrilling for geologists to later discover gold while on the hunt for chromium, nickel, copper, and zinc. They knew the Ring of Fire possessed many of the same characteristics as some of the world's great gold camps, including the age of its rocks, an abundance of iron, and the presence of major faults and fold structures. Younger sedimentary basins positioned next to older volcanic rocks looked suspiciously similar to the setting of the tremendously gold-rich Abitibi camp, about 750 kilometres to the southeast. Nevertheless, the actual discovery of the precious metal was happenstance in the Ring of Fire.

Accidental finds were to become a recurring theme in the camp: explorers looking for diamonds found copper and zinc instead; then they looked for copper and zinc and found nickel; looked for nickel and found chromite; looked for more of these metals and found gold. They were an indicator of just how extraordinary a mining camp, on a global scale, the Ring of Fire was turning out to be.

✳

The Ring of Fire's diverse array of mineral deposits is contained within what is called a greenstone belt, so named because of the dark green minerals in the bedrock. In northern Canada, most greenstone belts formed during the Archean Eon, beginning about 4 billion years ago and extending to the start of the Proterozoic Eon 2.5 billion years ago. The Nuvvuagittuq belt in Quebec, for example, has the oldest known rocks on Earth.

Greenstone belts occur along the crustal sutures where slabs of ancient continental crust collided or pulled apart and magma rushed to the surface. Canada's Abitibi greenstone belt, straddling the border between Ontario and Quebec, is one of the largest greenstone belts in the world, with a span of about 450 kilometres. Since the first mining camps were established there in the early 1900s, the belt has yielded 180 million ounces of gold, worth about US$350 billion at gold prices in 2022. Silver, copper, and zinc are also commonly found in economic quantities within VMS deposits in the Abitibi.

The McFaulds Lake greenstone belt, better known as the Ring of Fire, is at least 175 kilometres long and shaped like a bow or crescent. The belt is generally strongly magnetic and wraps around a granite pluton — an igneous body crystallized below surface — that later intruded from the depths, deforming the greenstone and giving it its distinctive ring shape.

Not only does the McFaulds Lake belt host large amounts of chromium, nickel-copper-PGE, zinc and gold, but it also contains potentially significant quantities of vanadium and titanium. The two metals, when combined in an alloy, have the best strength-to-weight ratio of any engineered material available today. Serious exploration of these types of deposits has yet to even begin.

It's hard to imagine another mining region with so many flavours. It's like combining the rich diamond pipes of Botswana with the high-grade chromite layers of the Bushveld complex in South Africa and the nickel-copper deposits of Michigan's Upper Peninsula, then mixing in the copper-zinc lenses of Manitoba's Flin Flon greenstone belt and the gold veins of the Abitibi: a Harrod's fruitcake of richness on a supersized scale.

"The wide diversity of mineral deposit types in the McFaulds Lake greenstone belt, including world-class Cr [chromium], significant Ni-Cu-PGE [nickel-copper-platinum group metals], and potential Fe-Ti-V [iron-titanium-vanadium] mineralization related to mafic and ultramafic rocks, make the Ring of Fire region an excellent exploration target to increase the world's supply of critical minerals," according to a Natural Resources Canada report on the region.[3]

Note the word "critical." Canada's biggest trading partner, the United States, is trying to secure minerals deemed essential to economic or national security (there are fifty of them, ranging from aluminum to zirconium) to avoid being cut off from supply as a result of geopolitics or other disruptions. Ontario is geographically close to U.S. automakers in Michigan and Ohio, and some of them have announced plans to manufacture electric vehicles that depend on some of these minerals at factories in the province. Other countries are also homing in. In 2022, South Korean battery manufacturer LG Energy Solution and European automaker Stellantis committed to build a C$4.9 billion electric vehicle (EV) battery plant in Windsor, Ontario, the first of its kind in Canada.[4]

Nickel, the dominant metal in the Eagle's Nest deposit and other deposits being evaluated in the Ring of Fire, increases the energy density of EV batteries so cars can run farther on a single charge. The International Energy Agency calculates electric cars require six times the mineral content of one running on an internal combustion engine. Likewise, copper, the other major component at Eagle's Nest, is sometimes called the "new oil" because of its role in capturing, storing, and transporting energy, including solar and wind energy. The red metal is essential to the arteries of the renewable energy system. Demand for both metals, according to commodity watchers, is forecast to rise steeply in the next decade.

And based on resource estimates and metallurgical studies, the Ring of Fire chromite deposits contain enough chromium to fulfill demand from North American stainless steel producers for fifty-eight years, and would potentially add C$2 billion to Canada's economy each year, according to earth sciences professor James Mungall, Noront Resources' chief geologist during the discovery phase of exploration.[5]

There is also a bounty of what explorers call "blue sky" exploration potential. The Ring of Fire lies within a much larger complex of rocks called the Oxford-Stull domain. This complex extends east-southeast from Manitoba all the way to north-central Ontario, where it dives below the Paleozoic sandstone and carbonate cover. Oxford-Stull contains other greenstone belts that wrap around granite domes just like the Ring of Fire.

Could there be more valuable mineral deposits lurking undercover somewhere else in this vast region?

CHAPTER 2

A Discovery in the Making

On one of those late September days that bask Toronto in a soft golden light, I cycle downtown to interview Neil Novak, the exploration geologist who first put the James Bay Lowlands on the proverbial map. Though we've likely crossed paths dozens of times at conferences over the years, we are formally meeting for the first time in 2019. Since 2007, the year of the Eagle's Nest nickel-copper discovery that set the market aflame, the in situ value of the metals discovered in the Ring of Fire has grown to tens of billions of dollars. But they remain stranded by a lack of infrastructure.

Novak gestures for me to sit across from his desk in a cramped, windowless office on the third floor of the Canadian Venture Building, a heritage site in downtown Toronto that's been converted into cookie-cutter rental offices. We are just getting into the guts of the Ring of Fire discovery tale when he reaches behind him and hands me an eight-inch-long cylinder of rock, split down the middle and polished to reveal the treasures within. The smooth, shiny, black drill core is a minuscule section of a much longer length pulled from under the swamps of far northern Ontario. The rock formed about 2.7 billion years ago, making it among the oldest on the planet.

My geoscientist eye has atrophied from lack of practice, but even I notice blotches of sulphide minerals mottling the background, a sign that the metal content, especially nickel, would be high. As previously mentioned, valuable mineralization of the kind resting in my hand forms when metals rain out of cooling magma that has ferried them to surface from the earth's mantle. The metals have an affinity for sulphur, so the two often end up together in high concentrations in the surrounding rock.

Novak points to the core sample. It's from drillhole NOT-07-01, which signalled the discovery of a lifetime in August 2007. "When we saw that," he says, "we knew we were at the base of a magma chamber and that pentlandite, the nickel mineral, was predominant."

When he says "we," he's including his colleague Howard Lahti. The two met thirty years before the discovery after Novak graduated from university with a B.Sc. in geology and they both found jobs in northern Quebec looking for uranium for the Australian company Pancontinental. Lahti was a strapping New Brunswicker of Finnish heritage known for his "sisu," Finnish for grit, guts, and tenacity. He had a Ph.D. in lithogeo-chemistry, meaning he knew his types of rock (lithos, from Greek) like no other. The two men worked well together on several projects over the decades. So Lahti was the first to get the call when Novak, by then serving as vice-president of exploration for Noront Resources, needed a competent exploration geologist to oversee the drilling project in what was soon to become known as the Ring of Fire.

Novak had been bitten by the mining bug as young as twelve, when he delivered the *Globe and Mail* to Horace Fraser in Palgrave, Ontario, in the 1960s. Unbeknownst to the paperboy, his client was president of Falconbridge Limited, one of the largest mining companies in the world at the time. On hot summer days, Fraser and his wife would invite Novak inside for a glass of lemonade at their grand farmhouse on the outskirts of town. There the boy would overhear stories of the mining magnate's latest travels to remote locales.

He grew even more intrigued by the sector when his father started working in the ready-mix concrete business. An affable, garrulous teen-ager, young Neil often got talking to the suppliers of sand and gravel arriving at the concrete plant where he worked summers. He was fasci-nated by the idea that the raw materials for concrete were transported from quarries of till left over by the last wave of glaciation. He decided to study science at university and was drawn to the geology program at the University of Waterloo.

A dozen years post-discovery, Lahti is recently deceased. But Novak has hardly changed. He still has the look of a southern U.S. gentleman, minus the western bowtie. His horseshoe moustache drops down neatly from his round face to blend into a modest grey beard that fans out across his chin.

He brings the conversation back to the unlikeliness of the Ring of Fire discovery. Successful exploration campaigns, a rarity in themselves, usually require several drill holes before valuable minerals reveal themselves. But because of the high cost of drilling (about C$100,000 per hole) in the remote, fly-in locale, Novak had only enough money in his budget for two. If those didn't hit pay dirt, he'd have to pack up his toys and go home to the exploration geologist's common curse — an uncertain future.

He remembers spotting the location of the first drill hole, NOT-07-01, about 20 kilometres west of Noront's exploration camp on McFaulds Lake, a slender body of water within the remote James Bay drainage basin. Shaped like an unshelled peanut, the lake spills into a river with no name that in turn feeds the Attawapiskat River flowing east to James Bay.

His drill target was a highly conductive and magnetic anomaly identified below the muskeg by an airborne geophysical survey designed to detect magnetic variations in rocks and pinpoint concentrations of potentially valuable metals. His exploration team had later zeroed in on the aerial hotspot by running a more detailed survey on the ground, feet shrivelling to prunes and freezing as they hauled a magnetometer through the swamp in a standard grid pattern.

Once Novak was satisfied he'd found the location with the best chance of a direct hit, he left the project execution in Lahti's hands and flew home. Lahti instructed the drillers to clear the bush from the area so a helicopter could sling in the necessary equipment.

Swatting away moose flies the size of bumblebees that were biting chunks out of his exposed flesh, Lahti calculated the correct drilling angle as the helicopter pilot lifted and nudged the drill left and right. Once the machine had settled in place, he told the drillers to set the drill at 45 degrees.

Late in the day on August 24, 2007, the drillers revved up the drill and water pumps. They started boring into the swamp overlying the bedrock, the acrid smell of diesel fuel tickling their nostrils, the whir of the diamond-studded drill bit meeting hard rock buzzing in their ears.

Once the drill was progressing as it should, Lahti hitched a ride back to camp in the chopper with the 7:30 p.m. shift change. He was probably wondering what chef Tony Laroche was cooking up in the kitchen tent that night. Would it be a camp favourite: slow-roasted prime rib roast, with gravy, mashed potatoes, and carrots? After the meal, Lahti might have time for a game of hearts or euchre, or even penny-ante poker if there were enough people up for it. The close quarters of the exploration camp made colleagues feel like family.

Later, satiated and succumbing to the kind of fatigue only a long day in the bush can induce, Lahti settled into his cot in the ten-by-sixteen-foot white canvas tent he sometimes shared with visiting geologists. He would have been lulled to sleep by the roar of the diesel generator in symphony with the steady hum of mosquitoes seeking the tiniest rent in the canvas that might lead to his flesh.

Although the late summer temperatures were already beginning to dip below ten degrees Celsius at night, the next day dawned fine and mild. Light winds generated in the mighty Hudson Bay to the northeast breezed across the flats, keeping the ferocious bugs at bay.

The day-shift drillers arrived on site around 8 a.m., curious to see what they would pull from the depths. But as the core emerged from the steel casing, it was looking more than a little dull: first, unconsolidated debris left behind by the glaciers followed by fractured limestone, then some broken-up sandstone overlying a pinkish, granite-like rock containing large crystals of quartz. Drilling through the unconsolidated and fractured rock on surface had been tough going. The drillers may well have been growing despondent in the middle of this vast, bug-infested swamp thousands of kilometres from home, wondering how they ever got there and when they could possibly leave.

But suddenly, about 50 metres down the hole and well short of the proposed target, the drill entered black rock studded with sulphide minerals that glittered in the daylight. The previous night shift had been pushing the hole hard, which tends to flatten the drill angle and explained the premature discovery. Recognizing the significance of the mineralization, the drillers radioed Lahti in camp so he could have a look and provide further instructions.

Lahti quickly saved the map he was working on, closed down his computer, and jumped back in the chopper to investigate.

As the drill was whirring, Novak was on a much-needed break from the bush, strolling down the main street of Frankenmuth, a faux Bavarian town in Michigan known for pretzel rolling and the world's largest Christmas store. He was shopping for clothes for the coming school year with his wife and two sons, keeping one ear cocked for the ring of his cellphone. Sure enough, the next buzz was Lahti dialling in from some 1,000 kilometres north on the camp's satellite phone. "We're into massive sulphides [mineralization consisting almost entirely of sulphides]. I'm seeing a lot of pentlandite [nickel sulphide] and the crystals are the size of my thumbnail," he exclaimed.

Novak knew by Lahti's description and the tenor of his voice that they'd hit the jackpot on their very first hole.

"I'll be there as soon as I can," he told Lahti, barely containing his excitement. "Drill a second hole at a steeper angle to undercut the first. That way we'll get a better idea of the true width of the mineralized zone."

Novak wasn't the only one to receive the news of the remote nickel discovery with Lahti's call, though he should have been. Exploration camps, especially ones with communal satellite phones like the one McFaulds Lake had, are notoriously leaky. Word had spread. Within days and without warning, a stampede of prospectors descended on Webequie, the tiny Ojibway community closest to the find. Novak fielded a lot of phone calls in those early days of the discovery, but the one he remembers most was from a bewildered Scott Jacob, then chief of Webequie, saying the remote community was overrun, three helicopters had just landed at their tiny airport, and the town's jet fuel was running dry. The sole motel was full and the Northwest Company Store, also the only one in town, was short of food.

The legal precedent that the Crown had a duty to consult and accommodate Indigenous groups when considering activities that might adversely impact their traditional lands, including mineral exploration, had been established in *Haida Nation v. British Columbia* three years previous in 2004.[1] But the Ontario government was nowhere to be seen as prospectors poured into the James Bay Lowlands.

"We have a six-room motel, each room with two double beds. People were sleeping in the hallways and the laundry room, paying the same rate as those in the rooms," Jacob told me. "The area of the Ring of Fire is huge [about 30 kilometres wide by 180 kilometres long], but people were running into each other in the bush. That's what you call a staking rush."

Luckily, Noront had scheduled the drilling for a weekend, so Novak had time to get back to Toronto to draft a press release before rumours of the find reached Bay Street, where speculation on the share price might rage out of control and trigger a trading halt by securities regulators.

On Tuesday, August 28, Noront announced publicly that the first hole of the program had intersected "visible copper sulphide mineralization in a pyrrhotite-chalcopyrite-peridotite geological setting." Pyrrhotite is iron sulphide. Chalcopyrite is copper sulphide. The host rock, peridotite, is a black igneous rock derived from the earth's mantle. Furthermore, the release stated, a second hole drilled at the same location — the one Novak had instructed Lahti to drill — had undercut the first and entered a similar, much wider zone of mineralization.

In a nod to the information breach that caused pandemonium in Webequie, the press release also declared that "unnecessary communication from the field camp has been curtailed and the local workers (drillers, pilots and First Nation workers) have been briefed on security measures . . . with respect to information discussion and release."

Investors knew what a huge deal it was to intersect such a large amount of base metal mineralization on the first drilling pass in a previously unexplored area. Noront's shares, which had been humming along at about 40 cents apiece, skyrocketed to 91 cents on the Toronto Venture Exchange. Within six weeks, junior companies and prospectors had staked tens of thousands of hectares along the ancient belt of green igneous rock that was soon to become known as the Ring of Fire. In their excitement, Noront's managers quickly agreed to fund two more drill holes — called step-out holes — east and west of the discovery to see how far the mineralization extended.

To their dismay, the core from both step-outs turned out to be barren. Could the intriguing discovery just be an isolated pod of base metals, too small to ever be economically viable to mine?

Keep the faith, insisted Noront president and CEO Richard Nemis. He flew north to investigate and prove the doubters wrong. He took John Harvey, former president of Noranda Exploration (a subsidiary of one of Canada's largest former mining companies), along with him to consult.

"I remember getting off the plane and going over to the core rack to look at the core. I came out with some pretty exciting language that I won't repeat," Harvey said later. "The massive sulphides reminded me of some of the [big mining] camps like Mattagami [in Quebec] and Bathurst [in New Brunswick]."

Putting his economic geology expertise to work, Harvey recommended another suite of holes to get a better sense of the size and direction of the mineralization.

On September 10, 2007, Noront issued a second release announcing the lab assay results from the first discovery hole: 36 metres of rock, longer than a basketball court, averaging 1.84 percent nickel and 1.53 percent copper. Even better, massive nickel and copper sulphides over 65 metres in width turned up in a fifth hole drilled nearly a city block away. Within days, Noront shares reached C$4 as word spread about the significance of the Eagle One (later named Eagle's Nest) find.

It was considered the best base metal discovery in Canada in a decade.

If you had invested C$10,000 in Noront in the early summer of 2007, your investment would have been worth C$100,000 by autumn. High risk for high reward: it's the fundamental nature of mineral exploration that attracts so many to the game.

✳

A whoop and the clink of glasses interrupt the steady hum of lunchtime conversation at Cyrano's restaurant on King Street East.

Toronto's mining community, especially its hard-drinking promoters and financiers, has been meeting at Cyrano's since 1959, shaking on deals and plotting their next exploration "play." On this autumn day in 2007, Nemis, Harvey, and financier Robert Cudney have gathered at the circular marble-topped bar in the middle of the dining room. The trio is huddled over a new map of the James Bay Lowlands, trying to conjure a catchy name for a crescent of volcanic rock in the middle of nowhere that promises such great riches.

"Look, the belt wrapping around the central geology looks like half of a ring," notes Cudney as he runs his index finger along the green shading on the map. He swivels his leather stool to face the others, his voice rising a notch. "And the magnetic highs are all lighting up in red. How about we call it the Ring of Fire?"

"Yes! That's it!" cries Nemis, a Johnny Cash fan who often mimicked the singer's signature wardrobe of all black. Hoisting his glass of red wine, he bursts into the musician's hit song, written by Cash's partner June Carter and Merle Kilgore but made famous by Johnny. Even though some scientists cringed at the flippancy of the Ring of Fire moniker, Richard Nemis was a promoter, not a geologist. He was smitten and he was the boss.

A few weeks after the Cyrano's gathering, shareholders shimmied into Noront's annual general meeting (AGM) in downtown Toronto to the tune of Carter and Cash's "Ring of Fire" booming from loudspeakers. By the end of October 2007, Noront's publicly traded penny stock had breached C$7 per share and Nemis was bragging about placing his next equity financing at C$10 per share.

"There have been many times when I was willing to say 'uncle' and quit this business," Nemis told his adoring shareholders at the AGM party. "But when it's all said and done you're doing it for exactly what happened with this little company of ours."[2]

The room erupted in cheers. Nemis had made a lot of people extremely wealthy with his nickel-copper discovery in the James Bay Lowlands — on paper at least.

✳

When it comes to mineral exploration, the label "promoter" can have negative connotations. Many a retail (non-professional) investor has been swindled by promoters who stake claims on ground with limited or no value — known in the business as moose pasture — and talk up the ground as if it were the next great mine. In the ensuing "pump and dump" scheme, they sell their shares, deflating the stock bubble before the trusting investor can cash in.

But promotion has a role in legitimate projects too. It's next to impossible to raise money for such a speculative venture as exploration without creating some market excitement around a play. Some research analysts who make their living evaluating the investment quality of junior mining companies — early-stage companies mostly involved in the exploration phase of mining and responsible for most of the world's mineral discoveries — won't touch even the most promising projects unless company management shows a flair for enticing investors.

In this regard, Richard Nemis was a pro. He was just the person to convince both retail and institutional investors to finance the kind of high-risk/high-reward drill campaign the Ring of Fire discovery required. And his timing was good: in 2007 the internet was just emerging as a popular platform for discussion and debate in the penny stock investment community.

"Dick [Nemis] was one of the first promoters to step into the internet world and make it work," David Graham, a former Noront vice-president, told me. "By attaching the Ring of Fire moniker to the discovery, he created a cachet in the emerging internet and investor hubs. It all came together to go viral every time the Ring of Fire was mentioned in a news release. That thing went everywhere."

Nemis even had names for his diamond drills to go along with the Johnny Cash theme. One was Johnny and two others were Vivian and June, after Cash's first and second wives. Large prints of the late superstars were taped to the sides of the rigs. When "Vivian" began to burn out, she was allegedly left on the side of a bush trail and used for spare parts.

I first met Nemis in the 1990s when I was on the editorial staff of *The Northern Miner*, then housed — printing press and all — on Labatt Avenue in a rundown and since gentrified neighbourhood of east Toronto. The weekly, which celebrated its 100th anniversary in 2015, was then known as the bible of the mining industry, and in some aging circles, it still is. The paper caters to both the industry and to investors. Back in the days when print journalism was king, readers knew to buy the shares of juniors mentioned on *The Northern Miner*'s back page and sell them when they reached the front page. Many a mortgage was paid off, dream cottage acquired, and Porsche driven off the lot using this investment strategy.

We reporters were forbidden from owning mining shares to avoid potential conflict of interest. The same was not true of the paper's management. Nemis was a long-standing friend of *The Northern Miner*'s publisher, Maurice "Mort" Brown. Once in a while Mort would dash wild-eyed out of his fancy office (equipped with a shower and napping couch), tap one of us in the cramped newsroom on the shoulder, and dispatch us to Nemis's offices to hear about the promoter's latest exploration play. We usually didn't mind. It was a chance to get away from the tricks being performed on johns in the parking lot outside our newsroom window and into the glamour of the downtown core, which had a way of sucking you in at 2 p.m. and spitting you out just in time for the last subway train, giddy with beer and possibility.

At first glance, Nemis seemed unassuming with his permed hair and ill-fitted suits wafting stale cigarette smoke. Then he'd start talking. Using a couple of maps on a wall and a pointer as props, Nemis could seduce just about anybody into a play he believed in. He made it sound so easy, even to trained geoscientists who should know better: find the right geology, send in prospectors to sniff out metal clues on surface, stake some claims, drill a couple of holes, and abracadabra, your C$10,000 investment would become C$50,000 or more. His retail investors adored him.

That everyman retail base, a less common breed of investor in the current environment of risk aversion and concentrated wealth ruled by institutions, was to become an important factor in the takeover battle for Noront that erupted more than a dozen years later.

"I was never interested in stocks or mining before I met Richard," Elaine Finley, his legal secretary for thirty-four years, told me. "But after listening to him at a few AGMs giving his yearly update, I would want to go out and buy the stock myself. He was just so convincing. He had a knack for choosing which properties to go forward with and he believed in people. Even though he was a lawyer himself, he did many deals on a handshake and he kept his word."

✴

Nemis was born in Sudbury, Ontario, in 1938 to descendants of Ukrainian immigrants. His mother had endured polio and became bedridden after childbirth when he was thirteen, forcing "Dickie" to care for his younger brother Terry and newborn sister Melody while his father worked. "He washed the floors and cleaned the house and looked after me. He was very protective of Terry," recalls Melody.

He was a wild teenager, riding motorcycles fast and getting into bar brawls on a Sudbury Saturday night. But a gentler side emerged when he was singing or playing piano, talents he inherited from his mother, Anastasia Maria Kuczma. Born in 1916 in Sifton, Manitoba, Anastasia, using the stage name "Chrissie," sang back-up for the likes of Louis Armstrong and big band legend Fletcher Henderson when the American celebrities ventured across the border and needed musicians.

Her eldest son had an equal proclivity for making money by innovative and sometimes mischievous means. Richard would pick the wild blueberries that flourished in the late summer, fill the bottom half of quart baskets with crumpled newspapers, cover them with a thin sheet of paper, then sell the berries at full quart price. Or take a few containers of shoe polish down to Sudbury's Belton Hotel in the west end, a watering hole for both miners and management, perch himself on the front steps, and offer shoeshines for a few cents apiece. Once he and another boy stole all the tools from his father's shed and sold them for cash.

Despite the shenanigans, he graduated first in his high school class and was accepted to the University of Ottawa. He later received his law degree from Osgoode Hall in Toronto and worked briefly as a lawyer representing a diversity of clients, including residents of First Nations communities in northern Ontario and allegedly even some motorcycle gang members based in Sudbury.

But the swashbuckling nature of mineral exploration and the excitement of discovery drew him like a magnet. He decided to try his hand at the financing side of the business. In 1983 he founded Noront Resources, naming the company after Noront Steel, a business his father James had established in 1945 in response to the Canadian mining industry's growing demand for steel products.

Nemis had a knack for backing promising mineral projects partly because he surrounded himself with talented exploration geologists, including John Harvey of the Cyrano's trio, Mining Hall of Famer Mac Watson, and Neil Novak, the first geologist to find base metals in the James Bay Lowlands. And he kept his ear to the ground.

He lived for a good staking rush. He was active in the Hemlo region of Ontario in the late 1980s, when gold was discovered there, jumped into the Voisey's Bay nickel staking frenzy in Labrador in the mid-1990s, then moved on to the Windfall Lake gold promise of northern Quebec in the early 2000s. So it was natural he would be sucked into the James Bay Lowlands play in its earliest stages.

John Harvey, who was soon named Noront's chief operating officer for his acumen, first met Nemis in the late 1980s when Noranda's Golden Giant mine near Marathon, Ontario, was gearing up to produce close to half a million ounces of gold (worth about US$900 million in 2022) per year. Harvey had been scouting for gold exploration opportunities that might provide future feed for the mine's milling facility. Nemis held some claims in the area through Central Crude Ltd., another junior company he controlled. He became friendly with Harvey. Working together, the two discovered the Eagle River gold deposit near Wawa. They had to defer production because of falling gold prices, but the mine was eventually opened by another company in 1996. More than a quarter of a century later, Eagle River was still going strong.

Nemis's daughter Jennifer recalls scrambling around the outcrops at Eagle River with her brother Richard Jr., picking up rocks they thought contained gold to show to their dad. Visible gold is rare in outcrops, so usually the yellow specks were pyrite, an iron sulphide otherwise known as fool's gold. "That's Leaverite," their father would tell them with a smile and a wink — as in "leave her right there."

The business partnership between Nemis and Harvey flourished and became a lasting friendship. A couple of times per year, Nemis would invite Harvey and an assortment of prospectors, geologists, promoters, and some of his former First Nations legal clients to a weekend at his beloved "lodge" — a collection of cabins on Kabenung Lake in the Mishibishu area of northern Ontario. In the springtime they would convene for the "International Fish Derby and Geological Seminar." In the fall there would be moose hunting. In both cases, there was red wine, and lots of it.

"Dick loved the company and he loved to be a host," Harvey told me. I guess what happened at Kabenung stays at Kabenung, because I couldn't get another word out of Harvey about those boys' weekends. But the thrill of finding mineral deposits and potentially creating new wealth for the country together surely cemented the bonds.

"Dad, along with a lot of the other old-school boys, got into the business because of the spirit of mining — the excitement of the find, staking claims, taking tons of risk," Jennifer said.

✳

During the fall of 2007, investor interest in the Ring of Fire grew more intense. An information luncheon co-sponsored by IBK Capital Corp., the investment banking firm that had raised millions for Noront's Windfall Lake gold project in Quebec and was responsible for much of the financing for the Ring of Fire play, immediately sold out. From 2007 to 2010, mining claims staked in the area tripled to 90,000 — each one representing a square roughly 1,600 metres by 1,600 metres (256 hectares). Noront formed joint ventures with many of the newcomers in the area to help finance their exploration and create the atmosphere of a bona fide rush on par with the historic mining rushes in Canada.

Nemis's superlatives fanned the flames.

"It is probably the biggest new discovery in Canada in the last ten years. That's how big it is. It's important. *Very* important," Nemis told the *National Post* in October.[3]

"The assay results we've drilled so far are spectacular," he told *Reuters* a few days later.[4] "You don't need many more than 5 million tonnes at that kind of grade to make one hell of a deposit."

Nemis completed his next financing in February 2008, selling 6.5 million units at C$4 each. Each unit consisted of one common share of Noront and one-half of a warrant (a warrant is the right to purchase shares at a specific price). It was a much more modest price than the C$10 per share he'd imagined. But Nemis still managed to raise C$26 million, a kingly sum for a junior company with no assets other than a few claims in the remote bush. Some big names in the business participated in the private placement (financing sold privately, mostly to chosen investors), including Robert McEwen, founder of the Goldcorp empire; Pierre Lassonde, another legend of the gold world and founder of Franco-Nevada Corporation; Eric Sprott, one of Canada's few billionaires, who has made most of his fortune investing in precious metals; and Ned Goodman of Dundee Bancorp.

Warren Irwin of Rosseau Asset Management was another one of the early investors. He would soon become a Nemis nemesis.

✳

Flush with cash, Noront kept up a fevered pace in the lowlands, drilling several more high-priority targets within a few kilometres of the Eagle One discovery. Much of this drilling took place in the depths of winter, when the frozen ground provided a more stable platform but daytime temperatures routinely dipped below minus-40 degrees Celsius, freezing exposed human flesh in a matter of minutes.

On February 25, 2008, a press release announced "EAGLE TWO HAS LANDED." Noront had encountered a new zone of massive sulphides two kilometres southwest of Eagle One, proving the original discovery was not a one-off but part of a larger system of mineralization, possibly the tip of the iceberg of a brand new mining camp.

IBK Capital's founder Bill White recalls golfing on the Wailea course in Maui that month when he looked up to see his wife, Gale, charging towards him in a golf cart, a piece of paper waving from her outstretched hand. Gale knew the "EAGLE TWO" press release was significant because Nemis had asked her to show it to her husband ASAP, but she didn't grasp what the headline meant for her personally. Bill sure did. After scanning the release, he said to her, "Honey, go out and buy whatever house you want in the Wailea area. We'll make it our winter home."

The market went wild. By the end of February 2008 — just six months after the discovery — the stock price reached C$6.95, and would soon top out at about C$8. "The potential over a seven-kilometre-strike length could be just as big or bigger than a Voisey's Bay," Nemis shouted to a representative for Agoracom, Noront's investor relations firm, over the din of a massive crowd — some of whom had slipped in uninvited — celebrating the Ring of Fire at an IBK luncheon on March 6, 2008. Voisey's Bay in Labrador, a major nickel operation, was discovered in 1993 and is still operating three decades later.

In a ceremony held at the Toronto Stock Exchange in June 2008, the venture arm of the exchange named Noront the top company in the mining space and presented Nemis with an award of recognition.

Even at Noront's remote Esker camp 1,200 kilometres to the north, everyone knew when the shares had had a good day, despite the lack of cellphone coverage at the time. The camp mascot was a stuffed dragon one of the crew had picked up at a garage sale. When prompted, the dragon sang Cash's famous tune. On the days that Noront stock closed higher than it opened, someone would push a button on the stuffie's stomach and half the camp would erupt in song. Even though exploration was still at the very early stages of drilling and sampling, there was a lot of singing going on in those golden days.

But the carnival atmosphere wouldn't last.

Trouble was brewing for Nemis. His proclivity for hyperbole and his spending spree in the James Bay Lowlands were making some of his shareholders nervous. Perhaps he sensed his days were numbered. He seemed on edge. Geologist Matt Downey, a fresh hire, just twenty-nine at the time, was fond of Nemis but remembers him shouting a lot.

"He'd yell across the office, 'Mark, get in here!' because he didn't really know me or my name yet. His secretary, Elaine, they'd been working together for years, but he would yell for her too whenever he needed something."

Noront's stock started to freefall. The entire world's financial system, including the markets, was crashing along with it. On September 29, 2008, the Dow Jones Industrial Average fell 778 points as defaults on mortgage-backed securities imploded, the largest point drop in history at the time. Risky junior mining stocks such as Noront took the biggest hit during this widespread crash as investors flew to the perceived safety of blue chips and other investments.

To add to Nemis's woes, Rosseau Asset Management — which had subscribed for a piece of C$26 million financing — was taking advantage of the depressed share price to plot an attack. A nasty proxy battle, in which of a group of shareholders joins forces to gather enough votes to force corporate change, ensued.

Rosseau's Warren Irwin told the *National Post*, "They have a hell of a good property and it's being squandered. And if we don't get a good board and good management in here, it will be a lot harder to raise money in this difficult environment. At the current burn rate, they're going to run out of cash in about seven months."[5]

On October 9, Rosseau filed a public document alleging that Noront had "squandered opportunities, wasted substantial monies on non-core properties [meaning the Windfall gold project in Quebec], diluted its interests through option agreements, and made exaggerated claims that have never materialized." The hedge fund managers proposed that shareholders oust almost all of the Noront board, including Novak, Harvey, and seventy-year-old CEO Nemis, in favour of their own slate of directors.

It is not uncommon for large and powerful new shareholders to usurp a company's board if they feel the current leadership is incompetent. But Richard Nemis had become a legend in the exploration world by then. It was unthinkable that he would be tossed from his own company. Was the takeover attempt, cloaked as a vote of no confidence, really a corporate raid designed to seize control of the Ring of Fire metal riches?

Keep the faith, Nemis reminded his shareholders, keep the faith. But on October 27, Noront issued a press release introducing a new slate of directors:

> The new board will . . . ensure that Noront's future is pursued in a balanced manner in the interests of all shareholders. In order to achieve this compromise and to facilitate a resolution that is in the best interests of all Noront's shareholders, Noront's current president and chief executive officer, Richard Nemis, has agreed to stand down as President, CEO and director . . . in recognition of his outstanding and pivotal contribution to the success of the Company to date, Mr. Nemis will be named Chairman Emeritus of Noront for life and will serve as a special advisor to the new Board.

Noront's annual general meeting took place in the TSX Broadcast Centre the next day. It was standing room only. Emotions were running high. IBK Capital's Bill White, who by that point had raised about C$95 million for Noront, and a total of C$139 million for companies exploring in the Ring of Fire, recalls security guards surrounding the glassed-in meeting room at the Exchange Tower and spread out on other floors of the building to handle any disruptive or violent behaviour. Though White was not allowed to cast a vote because of conflict of interest, "we sided with Dick in our hearts."

The vote to oust the board was close, with the incumbents allegedly securing a slight majority, but Nemis was forced to concede. "You can't go forward with a public company when half the people are gunning for you," White told me. "Maybe half are happy to try to protect you, but that's not workable in the long run."

The group from Rosseau Asset Management — allegedly named after a lake in the Muskoka region of Ontario where Toronto's super-elite have summer cottages — took control of the company Nemis had built from scratch. His loyal followers were unable to shield Nemis from the coup.

"It really hurt Dick, because [Noront] bore the name of the Sudbury company that his dad built and his brother grew," his friend, colleague, and fellow Ring of Fire promoter Frank Smeenk recalled at Nemis's funeral in 2019.

Although he held onto most of his Noront shares and was named chairman emeritus, Nemis was forced to cede control of the company and, along with it, not only the Ring of Fire discovery but the Windfall gold discovery in Quebec.

It wasn't the first time he'd met that fate. He'd been forced to walk away from the Eagle River deposit he nurtured alongside Harvey because of low gold prices, only to witness another company put the mine into production a few years later. And he'd sacrificed Noront's attention to Windfall in order to focus on the Ring of Fire. By 2022, Windfall was set to go into production long after Nemis abandoned his dream there.

"A sad part of Dick's history," Harvey said, "were the successes he had that he couldn't hold on to."

CHAPTER 3

Happy Accidents

Throughout most of its history, hardly anyone believed a diamond mine would ever be found in Canada. In fact, there is a popular maxim in France — "faux comme un diamant du Canada" (as fake as a diamond from Canada) — based on one of Jacques Cartier's expeditions to North America in the sixteenth century, when he mistook the quartz crystals he found near Quebec City for diamonds.

But geoscientists working for De Beers, a diamond monopoly since its inception in 1888 until the beginning of the twenty-first century, were confident they could debunk that long-accepted wisdom. They had seen the kinds of ancient stable rocks that underlie much of northern Canada in their global investigations before. They knew the geologic conditions were perfect for the formation and preservation of diamond deposits. They just had to find them — quietly.

After a couple of decades using stealth prospecting and proprietary exploration techniques, the South African diamond behemoth finally found its Canadian treasure in 1987. Student Brad Wood discovered kimberlite boulders on the Attawapiskat River, flowing east to James Bay, while fishing during a weekend break from fieldwork.[1] Kimberlite, an igneous rock originating in the upper mantle of the earth at depths of about 160 kilometres, sometimes takes diamonds along for the ride as it ascends through fractures in the crust as magma. The magma solidifies at surface, often as a carrot-shaped pipe containing diamonds worth up to hundreds of millions, even billions, of dollars.

The following year, De Beers geoscientists progressed a step further towards their goal. They found the bedrock source of the diamond-studded boulders, the equivalent of medical scientists finding the gene that causes a disease. But the famously secretive company — going by the name of Monopros in Canada — remained mum about the discovery, never letting on that it had a potential diamond mine in its clutches.

But there was one person who knew exactly what De Beers was up to: the late geophysicist Don MacFayden. The former World War II flying ace had designed airborne surveys to detect kimberlite pipes in South Africa, where De Beers and most of its mines were headquartered. That made him privy to some of the exploration secrets the diamond producer's employees otherwise kept under wraps. MacFayden's other not-so-secret weapon was the work he was doing under secondment to the Ontario government to identify areas of mineral potential in the lowlands before land was set aside for conservation.

MacFayden's airborne survey for Ontario identified the large cracks in the basement rocks underlying the lowlands. To him, they resembled giant spiders. He thought there was a strong possibility they could be conduits for diamond-rich kimberlites. And so, in 1991, when Canada's very first diamond mine was discovered northeast of Yellowknife in the Northwest Territories (not, to the chagrin of the brass at Johannesburg head office, by De Beers, but by a tiny but determined Canadian junior called Dia Met Minerals), MacFayden got to work, riding a tsunami of investor interest in diamond exploration and the riches that could be made on mining speculation. He had learned to love risk while flying dangerously low passes over the Atlantic seaboard looking for submarines with a magnetometer strapped to the belly of his seaplane. Taking a chance on the remote possibility of finding diamonds in the James Bay Lowlands seemed tame by comparison.

He could keep secrets as well as any De Beers employee. He hired his nephew to stake claims over the spidery crustal features he'd identified on his airborne survey. To avoid arousing suspicions that MacFayden himself was behind the work, the nephew registered the claims in his own name.

Who then did MacFayden recruit to do the dirty work of slogging around the swamp looking for kimberlites? None other than geologist Neil Novak, who would later play such an important role in the Ring of Fire discovery.

In order to fund the expensive and time-consuming venture, MacFayden and Novak formed a public company in mid-1992 to tap into Toronto's equity market. They called it Spider Resources after the spidery crustal structures MacFayden had identified with his airborne survey. To share the risk and the work of fundraising, Spider entered into a joint venture with another Toronto-based junior company called KWG Resources.

"At my first meeting with Don at his planning office in Mississauga he said, 'If you agree to this proposal and you work well with us, it's going to change your life," Novak recalls. "But you'll have to go down a particular path and it's going to be an adventure you're never going to forget.'"

✳

Fieldworkers on the ground in the James Bay Lowlands contend with particularly challenging working conditions. In winter, they must endure temperatures that dip below minus-40 degrees Celsius, frostbite a constant danger. Summer is even crueller. They face the worst the insect world can inflict. Only the permafrost beneath their feet prevents them from being consumed by the icy swamp. As a result, they are advised to keep three pairs of boots in camp — one on their feet, one drying out in camp, and another spare — to prevent their feet rotting from the outside in. Trench foot killed thousands of soldiers during World War I, when they fought in cold, wet conditions without extra socks or boots. The soldiers couldn't have known that the blisters and redness forming on the bottoms of their feet would eventually lead to gangrene.

But Novak knew the dangers. He wore a tie-up boot with a rubber lower and leather upper, his khaki canvas pants tucked inside. He rubbed dubbin into the leather a few times a week to keep them relatively waterproof. And he was grateful for the helicopter that could spirit him from rare outcrop to rare outcrop, avoiding the swamp altogether.

Like most Canadian geologists at the time, Novak didn't know the first thing about exploring for diamonds, so MacFayden arranged for him to meet some of the finest minds in the global business. The experts steered Novak towards New Liskeard, near the Ontario-Quebec border, where De Beers had once found diamonds in kimberlite but, true to its secretive nature, hadn't identified the rock as such in the government assessment files to avoid attracting attention. By the time Novak arrived on the scene, De Beers — deeming the find of no economic value — had allowed its mineral claims to lapse. Spider was able to swoop in, restake the ground, and redrill the anomaly. Novak hit the kimberlite easily, allowing Spider to publicly claim the first known discovery of diamonds in bedrock ever in the province of Quebec. The announcement did wonders for Spider's recognition by a stock market newly obsessed with the gems.

While Novak was receiving an education in diamond exploration, MacFayden tapped into the market excitement to raise the five million dollars he needed to fly another airborne geophysical survey in the James Bay Lowlands and launch an exploration program. As a key global character in the development of aerial surveys to search for magnetic rock, he confidently got to work on a fixed-wing system he could strap to a plane to detect kimberlite. He used the magnetic signatures of the kimberlite bodies already known to occur in the area to guide him. They stood out like sore thumbs on geophysical maps of the lowlands because they typically pierce through the non-magnetic limestone bedrock.

Soon enough, the company had several distinct targets to investigate.

Novak has vivid memories of drilling into his first bull's-eye target in the middle of nowhere in 1994. As predicted by MacFayden's geophysical survey, the drill hit the contact between the overlying (non-magnetic) carbonate rocks and the ancient Archean (magnetic) rock underneath at about 125 metres. Another 20 metres down the hole, the drill intersected what looked like kimberlite to Novak's newly trained eye. He called MacFayden with the news.

By then Novak was getting desperate for some civilization and family time after weeks of squashing bugs and squelching through the swamp, his mapping clipboard smeared with his own blood. Imagine his delight when he got his marching orders to go back to Toronto so that MacFayden and some kimberlite specialists could evaluate the core and determine its pedigree.

Novak's family picked him up at Pearson International airport. Instead of taking him home, they ferried Novak straight to Spider's new office in downtown Toronto, where he opened his backpack and retrieved the drill core. To put Novak's son Kyle at ease among the adults, MacFayden asked the four-year-old what he thought the mysterious piece of rock might be. Kyle said with confidence, "My daddy says it's kimberlite." To honour this bold statement, Spider named the pipe "Kyle" after the lab later confirmed that the ancient sample was indeed the potentially diamond-bearing rock.

Between 1994 and 1997, the Spider-KWG team discovered seven kimberlites by testing thirty-six targets. With a little luck and a lot of money, it seemed just a matter of time before the joint venture found a diamond mine of its own.

But suddenly the notoriously fickle venture market for mineral exploration stopped caring. In 1997 the Bre-X Minerals fraud — a gold scam perpetrated in Indonesia by a Canadian company — erased C$6 billion in shareholder value from the Toronto Stock Exchange. Investors lost their appetite for speculative exploration stocks. Spider and KWG fell into obscurity along with the rest of the junior mining market. It was a dark and dreary time for exploration geologists, many of whom found themselves out of work or driving school buses for income.

Novak took what money Spider had left in the treasury and tried to breathe some life into the company's shares by acquiring ground with the potential for diamond deposits in Brazil. But the Brazilian landowners weren't keen to negotiate, and, at times, Novak felt his life was in danger, so he retreated to Canada in 2000, just as the market was becoming more receptive to mineral exploration again.

Meanwhile, junior companies ignited by spectacular ongoing discoveries in the Northwest Territories (which eventually became Canada's first diamond mines) were still fanning across the nation, finding diamonds in several provinces. Upstaged in a country where they had been searching for decades, the executives at De Beers started making plans to put a diamond mine into production in the James Bay Lowlands. The Victor pipes were just two of sixteen diamond-bearing kimberlites De Beers had found in the area since their 1980s bedrock discovery. They appeared to show the most promise.

That turned out to be an understatement. The Victor diamonds were of unusually high quality, even by worldwide standards: a disproportionate number of gems, most with the shape and colour most sought after by jewellers, and with few impurities. By the time Victor closed in 2019 after an eleven-year run, De Beers estimated the mine had generated C$6.7 billion in GDP, including spin-off businesses and employment. In 2020 a single stone cut from a 271-carat rough diamond unearthed at Victor sold for US$15.7 million, a record price in an online auction. So much for "faux comme un diamant du Canada."

✳

De Beers was intrigued by Novak's Kyle kimberlite discovery because it was of Proterozoic age (541–2,500 million years ago), whereas all of the kimberlites they had found in the lowlands so far were of Jurassic age (146–200 million years). One of the largest diamond mines in the world — the Premier Mine in South Africa — is of similar vintage to Kyle. Because kimberlites usually form in clusters, De Beers wanted to investigate the potential for a separate Proterozoic grouping of diamond-rich deposits in the area to complement their much younger finds. The South African company offered to fund more drilling in exchange for a share of whatever Spider and KWG found. The trio formed a joint venture on February 28, 2001.

The joint venture had access to the data generated by MacFayden's airborne survey. But the players also had a secret weapon: proprietary geochemical techniques that could identify "indicator minerals" — minerals that tend to occur with diamonds — in soils and glacial till. By combining the two datasets, the partners were able to home in on a coincident geophysical and geochemical anomaly they thought had an excellent chance of representing a diamond-bearing kimberlite hidden at depth.

They started to drill.

In May 2002, as the drilling was progressing, Novak was meeting with the Ontario Geological Survey in Timmins to update them on the enticing project. Unexpectedly, he received a call from Deirdre O'Donohoe, De Beers' project geologist, who was managing exploration for the joint venture. Novak was just about to switch to speakerphone so that Don Boucher, a De Beers exploration manager also attending the meeting, could hear. But O'Donohoe advised him to step outside with Boucher instead. When they did, the two geologists were dumbfounded by the news: instead of intersecting kimberlite, the hole had cut through a thick wedge of copper and zinc mineralization.

The lab later confirmed an intersection of about eight metres with a grade of 1.61 percent copper, including a half-metre section running 7 percent copper and almost 5 percent zinc. The spectacular and surprising results drew attention — for the first time in history — to the base metal promise of the area, especially the potential for volcanogenic massive sulphide deposits. As explained earlier, these deposits are metal-rich lenses formed from hot lava pouring out from vents along fault lines in the seafloor, creating so-called black smokers that geologists continue to find at the bottom of oceans today. Canada hosts about 350 of these deposits. They collectively produce large quantities of zinc, copper, silver, and gold.

The Spider-KWG joint venture would go on to discover ten such occurrences in the James Bay Lowlands. But by 2002, the market for mineral exploration ventures had once again sailed into the doldrums. Investors barely noticed the extraordinary discovery, and Novak did his best to keep the location quiet to avoid competition.

There are advantages to the wildly cyclical market for mineral exploration financing that, for the most part, correlate with commodity price swings: if you think you've got a winner and you have a little money saved up, you can use slow periods to assemble a package of claims and/or test out exploration theories and techniques. Then when the market turns hot again — as it always does — you're already ahead of the game. So Novak wasn't completely discouraged by the lack of market excitement.

De Beers' managers only had eyes for diamonds. They ceded their interest in what had become a copper-zinc project to Spider and KWG. And exploration in the James Bay Lowlands — so far from any roads or other infrastructure — was once again perceived by the general market to be an exercise for the reckless or foolhardy.

✳

But at least two people spotted the press release announcing the Spider-KWG base metal discovery, considered the results highly significant, and acted upon their instincts. One was Richard Nemis. He had just raised millions to explore the Windfall gold property in Quebec on the basis of a spectacular drill intersection of visible gold over a width of about five metres. He decided to redeploy some of that cash to seize ground near the Spider-KWG metal find and launch an exploration program. The other was Mac Watson, president of Freewest Resources and a geologist with the Midas touch.

"I ran into Neil [Novak]," Watson told me later, "and I said, 'Neil, I know where you are working up there, and I can send my [claim] stakers in to compete with you, or you can give me your stakers when you're finished.'" They shook on the latter.

It just so happened that Watson and Nemis both owned condominiums on the Gulf Coast of Florida. They agreed to fly Novak down to the Sunshine State to map out the claim blocks. One November day in 2002, Novak arrived at Nemis's light-filled condo with a map roll slung under his arm. It was a welcome contrast to the gloomy chill of the lowlands. The three middle-aged adventurers, along with Spider president Norm Brewster and consultant Wayne Ewert, grabbed themselves a beer, rolled out MacFayden's giant geophysical map on the living room floor, and anchored the map with bottles. Though claim staking and exploration can be a competitive business, the necessary expense of using helicopters to secure ground in the James Bay Lowlands encouraged cooperation among the rivals.

They zeroed in on the magnetic anomalies that were still open for staking and began to strategize. Freewest didn't have much money in the kitty, so could afford only a few claims. But Noront was able to tap into the millions it had just raised for the Windfall property to stake a bigger chunk and mobilize drills to the site. Mum was the word.

"The lack of interest [in mineral exploration at the time] gave us a moat around the business that kept others out," explained IBK Capital's Bill White, who had always kept the faith in Nemis and had spearheaded the financing for Windfall and, later, the Ring of Fire. As a token of his appreciation for the oodles of money they made for him, White would later present Nemis, Watson, and other members of the discovery team with copies of *The Little Engine That Could*, a classic tale used to educate children about the rewards of perseverance and optimism.

Nemis soon had another source of capital to finance his ambitions: Robert Cudney, the Toronto financier who later suggested the "Ring of

Fire" name. As Cudney tells it, he was settling into business-class seat 1A on a flight home from Vancouver when Nemis took the seat beside him. Cudney did not know Nemis well, but over drinks on that five-hour flight, he heard of the huge mineral potential of the James Bay Lowlands. Cudney was sold on the idea. On a handshake, he offered to put C$400,000 into the speculative play in exchange for shares in Noront. It was the beginning of a long partnership for the two risk-takers.

Once the Florida group had amicably divvied up the best ground, Novak flew back to Ontario to quietly set up a staking camp on McFaulds Lake. His stakers managed to secure twenty-five claims for Noront and nine for Freewest before the region plunged into winter deep freeze. But Freewest didn't have any money left for drilling, and the market had no interest in helping out. Even Novak was growing discouraged. Base metal prices were slumping, other companies drawn to the area were giving up, and Spider was once again having trouble raising money for exploration.

Was it time to turn his attention back to diamonds?

✳

It was around this time that Frank Smeenk entered the picture and took the reins at KWG as president and CEO. Smeenk, the eldest of nine children, is a lapsed lawyer like his late friend and colleague Richard Nemis. He studied law at the University of Western Ontario in his hometown of London in the early 1970s and was admitted to the Law Society of Upper Canada in 1976. He was drawn to the mining industry in 1987 after helping to restructure a New York–based commodity-trading firm that held some dormant mining assets.

He later told the *National Post*, "In the back of my mind I was always looking for an opportunity to do business. In [a] perfect world Labatt [the beer dynasty] would have plucked me out of my law practice and made me president."[2]

Smeenk instead took control of MacDonald Mines Exploration Ltd. (and its sister company MacDonald Oil Exploration Ltd.), a defunct junior that had first listed on the stock exchange in 1939. He decided to try his luck in Cuba. He used Toronto equity markets to finance millions of dollars of exploration for gold and oil there. He even sat on an international trade advisory board in the communist nation.

But in 1996, Cuba shot down two American planes just as gold prices were falling. And a year later the collapse of Bre-X Minerals, one of the biggest mining frauds of all time, put an abrupt stop to the flow of easy money for mineral exploration globally. MacDonald Mines, like thousands of other junior mining companies, almost went belly up.

Smeenk saw opportunity in the Bre-X collapse. After the Canadian company exploring in Indonesia was declared a fraud, he tried to acquire two of Bre-X's sister companies, Bro-X Minerals and Bresea Resources. Both were under court protection from creditors, but between them they hoarded several millions in cash. Smeenk intended to liberate their treasuries to finance his Cuban exploration dreams.

Then, in 1999, he made a run at the Cuban unit of Saxton Investments Ltd., a Canadian investment firm that allegedly misappropriated millions of dollars of investor money. Smeenk said at the time that MacDonald Mines' previous experience in Cuba made the company "an ideal vehicle to turn the clients' original investments into listed securities."[3]

His failed attempts to take over these tainted assets were a red flag for the Ontario Securities Commission (OSC). On closer investigation, the regulator found that Smeenk and his companies had ignored financial disclosure requirements for years. In early 2001, Smeenk admitted to conduct that contravened securities laws. The OSC ordered him to cease trading in all securities for a year, limited his ability to serve on the board or management of MacDonald Mines, and fined him C$5,000.[4]

Later that year, major mining company Falconbridge called off a joint venture agreement with MacDonald Mines to explore a platinum project in Ontario because of "regulatory and environmental concerns" with the proposal.[5]

Smeenk went quiet after the OSC wrist slap, though he was still a director of some junior mining companies, including James Bay Lowlands explorer KWG Resources. In 2004, he was elected KWG's president and CEO.

✳

Despite the lack of interest from the market in the area that came to be known as the Ring of Fire, the three associates — Novak, Smeenk, and Watson — decided there was enough strength in numbers and a chance to keep going despite the odds. At the end of 2005, Spider and KWG agreed to explore Freewest's claims in exchange for earning an interest in them.

Their first pass was, once again, a happy accident of discovery. On March 6, 2006, Hole FWR-06-03 hit not copper-zinc as expected, but massive chromite over a couple of metres with some platinum and palladium in the mix. They called the discovery Big Daddy.

Chromite ($FeCr_2O_4$) is used to make ferrochrome, a key ingredient in stainless steel manufacturing. But chromium — the brittle, lustrous steel-grey metal derived from chromite and valued for its corrosion resistance — isn't a well-understood commodity in Canada. Besides, the grades at Big Daddy weren't initially all that spectacular compared to the better-known Bushveld Complex of South Africa, where grades reach nearly 50 percent. The partners decided to shelve the project. Watson turned his attention to other, more achievable exploration projects outside of the James Bay Lowlands.

The Big Daddy chromite discovery was not so surprising in a geological sense. As described earlier, when magma cools as it rises from the mantle, metals drop out in layers. Chromite crystals are the heaviest and sink to the bottom, while sulphides rest above the chromite layers. In the case of the Ring of Fire, the rocks have been twisted and overturned by subsequent folding and faulting and so appear to be upside down (with the chromite closer to surface), but the magmatic sequence is classic.

In 2007, when Noront set the market ablaze with its Eagle's Nest nickel discovery, Watson had a change of heart. He decided the time was ripe to revisit the metal potential of claims Freewest held outside the partnership with Spider and KWG. Some would suspect his efforts of "closeology," the practice of taking advantage of proximity to a new discovery to pump one's own stock price, but Watson wasn't inaugurated into the Canadian Mining Hall of Fame for nothing. He knew he had some juicy magnetic conductors on the ground he had secured at the Florida retreat. They warranted investigation, especially during a newly receptive market for exploration financing.

In his eighties, Mac Watson is still a going concern in the exploration business when he arrives at my doorstep in the pouring rain one October morning in 2019. He's between meetings in Toronto on his way back from the Sudbury area, where he'd been investigating a promising gold project with his finely honed eye. As we meet over coffee at my dining room table, his phone rings repeatedly. Before the hour is up and I can blurt out another question, he's got his leather jacket on, ready to bolt back downtown on the subway for another meeting before hopping on a plane back to his home in Montreal.

He and John Harvey — the exploration manager from Noranda, former Noront executive, and dear friend of Richard Nemis — have recently returned from their sixtieth reunion at the University of New Brunswick, the only two geologists from UNB's 1959 graduating class to fly to Fredericton for the occasion. Harvey, the city slicker from Toronto, and Watson, the country boy from a farming community in Quebec, found themselves in the same class at UNB and have been friends and business associates ever since.

Watson's father was a veterinarian and a descendant of Scottish immigrants who settled in the rich farmland of southwestern Quebec. The elder Watson had an interest in penny stocks and was a loyal subscriber to *The Northern Miner*. The thrill of the volatile junior mining market his father read about in those pages rubbed off on young Mac.

Watson was equally drawn to the outdoors, so when he found himself bored and restless while studying physics at Bishop's University in Quebec, he enrolled in the geology department at UNB with an eye to igniting the kind of exploration plays his father liked to gamble on. He continues to believe that Canada has some of the most attractive geology in the world for economic deposits and has done his best work east of the Manitoba border, including discovering the Holloway gold mine near Kirkland Lake, Ontario.

Dressed casually in dark pants and a black Ralph Lauren V-neck that contrasts splendidly with his shock of thick white hair and eyebrows, he thinks back to his 2007 exploration program in the James Bay Lowlands, one of dozens he has overseen in his fifty-plus-year career.

"After the Noront hit, we cut our lines, did our ground geophysics and put a camp in there," says Watson, who was the first to run gravity surveys, which measure the density of rock, to detect massive sulphides in the Ring of Fire. "We were in there to really explore this time. We started drilling and on the first hole I remember [project geologist] Don Hoy calling me from the bush on a Sunday afternoon. . . . I knew that if he called on a Sunday, it must be important. So I asked, 'How much nickel do you see?' Don said, 'I don't see any nickel, but I do see 100 metres of massive chromite.'"

Watson's eyes begin to twinkle and his mouth turns up in a multi-million-dollar grin as he continues: "I was thinking, What the hell am I going to do with chromite? But I was pretty happy because it was high grade and I thought maybe it would be worth something."

Sure enough, Freewest moved the drill 1.7 kilometres along strike, or trend, of the geology — a very big step-out for an exploration program — and hit another 100 metres of high-grade chromite. Freewest had just discovered the largest and richest chromite deposit in North America. The Ring of Fire chromite play, in conjunction with the nickel-copper play, was on. Freewest called the discovery Black Thor. Another parallel deposit discovered to the northwest of Black Thor was named Black Label.

It seemed only a matter of time before a major company came calling.

※

In March 2010, Watson joined Neil Novak, Richard Nemis, John Harvey, and Don Hoy (who ran the chromite exploration programs) to receive the Prospectors & Developers Association of Canada's Bill Dennis Award for their work in the Ring of Fire. The national award, considered one of the greatest honours globally for an exploration geologist, recognized their discoveries — those happy accidents of chromium, copper, nickel, and zinc — under difficult conditions. The award also acknowledged their role in opening up a previously overlooked area of the country to new exploration activity.

At a gala ceremony held at the Royal York Hotel in Toronto, where Nemis and the others accepted the award, he told the audience: "My heart will always belong to northern Ontario. It gives me great pleasure to see the potentially enormous economic boost the Ring of Fire discovery will have on the north, on Aboriginal communities, and hopefully on Sudbury's world-class mining supply and service industry." In his characteristically boosterish fashion, Nemis added: "In fact, I think the Ring of Fire will rival the Sudbury basin and the economic impact of this discovery on the Ontario economy will probably run into the hundreds of billions of dollars over time."

Would Nemis's spectacular dream ever come true? Developments over the next decade would suggest otherwise.

CHAPTER 4

Cliffs Comes Calling

There are a couple of thousand junior mining companies in Canada just like Novak's Spider Resources or Nemis's Noront. Most of them are listed on the Toronto Venture Exchange, where they go cap in hand for funding to support their global exploration efforts. Often consisting of no more than one or two exploration geologists or promoters, these tiny enterprises are the lifeblood of mining in Canada and elsewhere.

They are called penny stocks because they literally trade for pennies until they make a strike worthy of the market's attention. If the stars align — management has a track record of discovery; the project is deemed to have potential; and commodity prices are on a cyclical upswing — these juniors can raise millions of dollars on the stock market in a matter of weeks. On the other hand, when commodity prices are depressed or the market is in a slump for other reasons, many simply become zombie companies on the exchange or delist altogether.

Nimble and innovative, they are the antithesis of the slow-moving behemoths — multinational miners such as Barrick or Anglo American — that sit atop the mining food chain. And juniors have made most of the world's mineral discoveries. A suitable analogy would be biotech start-ups working in research labs to develop new drugs for the pharmaceutical sector. Both are high-risk ventures, but they also can be highly rewarding financially in the rare instance they succeed.

When juniors make an enticing discovery of gold, diamonds, or other potentially economic minerals, their major counterparts, the mine operators, are usually interested in having a look at the drilling and sampling data, if not buying the junior outright. Mineral deposits require replacement on a regular basis because mines simply run out of ore, sometimes within a decade or less. The only way for a mining company to survive is to build a pipeline of future mines, either by making new discoveries or acquiring someone else's. Majors are almost always better off choosing the latter option; the risk-reward dynamic of exploration is poorly understood by their shareholders, and their top-heaviness tends to make them lousy explorers.

So it was no great surprise when Cliffs Natural Resources, the oldest and largest mining company in the United States, jumped into the Ring of Fire with both feet in 2009. Cleveland-based Cliffs had been strategizing about how to branch out into the ferrochrome industry from its core business of mining and processing iron ore and coal to make steel; access to a supply of chromite would allow Cliffs to take the steelmaking process one step further by producing ferrochrome, an alloy required to manufacture stainless steel.

The ingredient they needed to complete the plan was chromium. The metal is common in the earth's crust but is usually bound up in chromite, a mineral composed of 42–56 percent chromium. To produce ferrochrome, chromite is reduced with carbon in a furnace to form an alloy with a 2:1 chromium-to-iron ratio. Add in a little more iron for strength, some nickel for pliability, and a dash of manganese to bind the other materials together and voilà, you've got stainless steel: a strong, versatile material that resists corrosion and microbial contamination, making it useful in everything from construction to surgery.

According to Roskill, a U.K.-based metals and minerals research group, the growth of the stainless steel market has outpaced lead, copper, zinc, aluminum, and carbon steel markets over the past three decades. China is the world's largest producer of both ferrochrome and stainless steel but hosts no known chromite resources of its own. As a result, its growing economy has a voracious appetite for foreign chromite supplies.

The value of chromium consumption in the U.S. alone is about US$1 billion per year, mostly from imports. In 2018, the U.S. Department of the Interior placed chromium on the list of metals and minerals it considers "critical." The country aims to have a "secure and reliable" supply of these commodities. But the world's biggest supplier of chromium by far is South Africa, followed by Turkey and Kazakhstan. Supply from these regions is vulnerable to geopolitical tensions and shipping challenges, making any new North American supply of great interest to the American government.

✳

By mid-2009, Spider Resources, KWG Resources, and Freewest Resources were drilling to determine the extent of Big Daddy, the chromite deposit Neil Novak's team had inadvertently uncovered three years earlier while they were looking for copper-zinc sulphides. But KWG was running out of money to fund its share of the exploration costs. The junior would need to go back to the stock market to raise more funding, cede part of its share of Big Daddy, or appeal to a larger partner for support.

As it happened, one of KWG's directors, Michael Harrington, was an American mining executive and an acquaintance of Cliffs' president. He set up a meeting in Cleveland between two representatives of Cliffs, Richard Fink and Bill Boor, and KWG president Frank Smeenk. Securing control of the Ring of Fire chromite deposits made strategic sense to Cliffs because it was an opportunity to develop and operate the first mine-to-smelter ferrochrome business in North America. It was an irresistible temptation for an ambitious miner primed for growth.

To get a close, confidential look at the data the juniors had collected with their sampling, surveying, and drilling, Cliffs bought small interests in Freewest, KWG, and Spider, the trio of juniors that controlled Big Daddy. Freewest also owned the Black Thor and Black Label chromite deposits Watson and Hoy had discovered to the northeast along the same 14-kilometre trend.

Cliffs liked what it saw. The big company named KWG its junior partner and placed Richard Fink on the board of KWG to represent its interests. Cliffs then put plans in place to take over the juniors and wrest 100 percent control of Big Daddy, Black Thor, and Black Label and develop a multi-billion-dollar mining and processing operation.

But the American company had a fight on its hands. The new management of Noront, installed in 2008 after the proxy battle in which Nemis and his colleagues were dethroned, had launched a hostile takeover bid for Freewest to consolidate exploration properties in the Ring of Fire. The proposed deal offered one Noront share for every four Freewest shares, valuing Freewest at approximately C$90 million. "[Noront] tried to sweet talk us into doing a merger over dinner at a steakhouse in Toronto," Mac Watson of Freewest revealed later. "I said I'd think about it, but we didn't really want to do it."

When Noront announced the hostile bid to the public, Freewest warned its shareholders the offer was "highly opportunistic and significantly undervalues Freewest's assets." A bidding war ensued. Cliffs swooped in with an offer to buy Freewest for C$150.6 million. Noront counter-offered. In the end, Cliffs won the day, acquiring Freewest in January 2010 for C$240 million, or C$1 per share. It was a lot to pay for a handful of remote, unproven resources, but Cliffs was determined to sweep the feisty juniors out of the way so it could control the camp unencumbered.

"The acquisition of Freewest is consistent with our strategy to broaden our geographic and mineral diversification and allows us to apply our expertise in open-pit mining and mineral processing to a chromite ore resource base that could form the foundation of North America's only ferrochrome production operation," Cliffs said in corporate update later that year. "The planned mine is expected to produce 1 million to 2 million [tonnes] of high-grade chromite ore annually, which would be further processed into 400 thousand to 800 thousand [tonnes] of ferrochrome."

To put those numbers in context, South Africa produces 15 to 20 million tonnes of chromite annually, or about 60 percent of global production, and hosts three-quarters of the world's undeveloped chromite reserves and resources.[1] So Cliffs' proposed output wouldn't come close to South Africa's contribution, but it wasn't a drop in the bucket either. The proposed production would meet about a quarter of U.S. demand.

Watson was happy too because he was able to spin off all of Freewest's non-chromium assets, which Cliffs didn't want, into a brand new Freewest. His spin-off company would go on to make additional discoveries, including a rare-earths deposit at Strange Lake in Quebec near the Labrador border.

Next in the American powerhouse's crosshairs were KWG and Spider, which each had a 26.5 percent stake in Big Daddy. KWG's management had been hoping to remain Cliffs' preferred partner in the Ring of Fire, doing the tough work on the ground while Cliffs took care of the higher-level negotiations and financing. But even though Cliffs had a representative on the KWG board, the bigger company wasn't interested in partnering. It wanted complete control. "[Cliffs] didn't really want very much to do with me," Smeenk told me later. "Maybe it was me, personally. I don't know. But they never took any of my advice."

Novak recalls that on Canada's May "two-four" weekend in 2010, Cliffs executive Bill Boor called him from Cleveland and offered eight cents per share for Spider. Boor said he would be making a separate offer for KWG in order to secure the share of Big Daddy that Cliffs hadn't acquired through its purchase of Freewest.

After some back and forth, Cliffs offered to pay 13 cents per share in cash for each company, valuing KWG at C$100 million and Spider at C$86 million. In the years since its discovery in 2006 — the year before the Nemis nickel-copper hit that catapulted the region to fame — Big Daddy had proven to be large and rich in chromite, with grades averaging about 30 percent chromite. Naturally, KWG and Spider coveted their find.

In an attempt to keep control of Big Daddy, Smeenk started a bidding war for Spider by offering to merge with his joint venture partner. It was a war cash-poor KWG simply could not win but that nevertheless put a fire under the market price for Spider. Shareholders started exercising their Spider warrants — their right to buy shares of the junior at a specific price that was now lower than the market price — automatically putting them in the money. Spider's treasury was fortified. Smeenk must have been salivating over the resulting windfall, but he could not outbid Cliffs. Cliffs eventually swallowed Spider for 19 cents per share, or about C$125 million.

KWG was left jilted at the altar.

✳

But Smeenk had another trick up his sleeve. While Cliffs was still dipping its toes in the lowland swamps, he had had a brilliant idea. The Ring of

Fire operators needed a means to ship ore from any future mines but were completely cut off from transport infrastructure. The swamp did not lend itself to road or railway building. Wouldn't it make sense to secure control of the high ground leading from the nearest railway line to the mining camp as a potential transportation corridor?

Studying the maps and geology, Smeenk recognized a north-south trending esker, a glacial deposit left behind after the last retreat of glacial ice from the area thousands of years ago. It would make the perfect high ground for a railroad. Although certainly unconventional, it wasn't illegal under the Ontario Mining Act to stake mining claims for the purposes of transportation. So Smeenk set his sights on the 328-kilometre gravel ridge leading north from the CN railroad near Nakina to the Ring of Fire and deployed a team of claim-stakers to tie up the ground.

Cliffs had had the same thought. It knew that in order for its ambitious plan to work, the company would need a way to get the ore from the remote swamp to a processing plant in one of Ontario's northern cities. Cliffs supported KWG's staking in hopes of building a 340-kilometre-long rail spur, partially funded by Ontario taxpayers, to tie into the existing CN railway line running east-west to the north of the Lake Superior city of Thunder Bay.

But the relationship between Cliffs and KWG had soured over the battle for Big Daddy. And at some point, Cliffs changed its mind about the mode of transport, deciding that a road would be the less expensive and more feasible option than a railway for transporting ores and concentrate. Cliffs wanted the route to run along the high ground of the esker, but Smeenk refused to grant access. The animosity escalated.

Meanwhile, few were paying attention to what the First Nations communities needed or wanted. The lack of understanding about their legal rights amid the corporate pissing matches was beginning to weigh on Ontario premier Kathleen Wynne. "Cliffs was very ambitious," she told me later. "I felt worried about the degree to which some people in our government felt like the company could drive the process. I would always say that if we don't build the [community] relationships, nothing is going to get built. There were people around the table who didn't get that."

In 2012, Cliffs applied to Ontario's Mining and Lands Commissioner asking the regulator to overrule KWG's objections. The hearing took more than a year, and to the surprise of many in the industry, the commissioner denied Cliffs' application, affirming that a mining claim holder has prior right-of-surface use. It was one of many setbacks for Cliffs and for the Ring of Fire in general, and probably the last straw for those running the Cliffs show in Cleveland.

"I could tell there would never be a mine built," said David Anthony, an experienced mine-builder who was hired as a Cliffs VP and senior project director for the Ring of Fire at the end of 2010. "I said to Bill [Boor], 'This thing is not going to happen and I don't want to draw a salary doing nothing.' I told him this was just an exercise in swimming across the ocean."

Aside from the hundreds of millions the company was pouring into the Ring of Fire, in 2011 Cliffs also purchased the Bloom Lake iron ore mine on the Quebec-Labrador border for US$4.3 billion. The purchase was part of Cliffs' strategy to reduce its dependence on U.S. customers and boost its iron ore exports. At the time, iron ore prices were flying at all-time record highs of close to US$190 per tonne, compared to just US$30 per tonne in 2003. Producers worldwide were making a killing. With annual revenues of US$4.7 billion in 2010, Cliffs had been added to the Fortune 500 list. Management was oozing confidence and optimism. What could go wrong?

But higher-than-expected costs at Bloom Lake, coupled with a rapidly declining iron ore price, cut into Cliffs' earnings almost immediately. By the third quarter of 2012, the company's net income had dropped to US$85.1 million from US$601.2 million during the same three-month period a year earlier. Cliffs delayed a planned expansion at Bloom Lake and later registered a US$1 billion goodwill charge — applied to a company's books when the carrying value of an asset exceeds its market value — on the purchase price of the iron ore mine.

But the damage had been done. The losses were mounting, and Cliffs' love affair with Canada was turning toxic. In a single day in February 2013, its share price dropped 20 percent to US$30, signalling that shareholders were fed up with Cliffs' poor judgment on the Canada file. The company earned the dubious honour of second-worst-performing stock on the New York Stock Exchange that year.

In mid-2013, amid shareholder rumblings over its botched Canadian investments, Cliffs fired president and CEO Joseph Carrabba and president of global operations Laurie Brlas. Gary Halverson, a Sudbury native, replaced Carrabba at the helm. But Halverson lasted less than a year. Cliffs sacked him too after Casablanca Capital, a New York hedge fund and key shareholder, won a proxy battle in the boardroom and installed one of their own, Lourenco Goncalves, to run the company. Goncalves promptly declared that the Ontario mineral deposits had "zero hope" of being developed in his lifetime.

The Cliffs team on the ground was crushed. "I don't think you can imagine how committed our team was to the chromite project because of the huge, positive social and economic returns," Richard Fink told me. "Guys were in the office until 11 p.m. during the prefeasibility study, and it took a personal toll.

"In my 46-year career, there was never any other project like this. At current ferrochrome prices, Cliffs' chromite [division] would be throwing off C$1.5 billion in annual revenue. Just think what that could be doing for the First Nations, northwestern Ontario, and the province as a whole. This was a complex, expensive project with a long lead time. But instead of focusing on the benefits, everybody wanted money upfront without taking any risks or giving us a firm timeline."

After buying three chromite deposits for C$350 million and spending about C$200 million on development, Cliffs abandoned its Ring of Fire properties. The crackling Ring of Fire had become a smouldering dung heap.

CHAPTER 5

The Little Junior That Could

Noront Resources owes its origins to the burst of enterprise following World War II. In 1945, Jim Nemis and some of his co-workers from the Sudbury nickel mining operations recognized the growing demand for fabricated steel in Sudbury and environs. They founded Noront Steel to meet that demand.

It was a typical entrepreneurial story: identify a need, formulate a plan to meet that need, start small in your buddy's garage, expand quickly as the contracts start rolling in, establish a consistent clientele. Aside from producing everyday wires and cables, Nemis Sr. had some fun designing the "Snowbug" snowmobile that hit the trails in 1969 and later became a collector's item. The Canada Science and Technology Museum describes the bug as "a fun loving recreational winter vehicle. Its three colours, bright orange, pale green and gold fleck gave it a truly unique and romantic look."

Jim's passionate heart failed in 1978, but his legacy lives on. In 2020, Noront Steel celebrated its 75th anniversary as a supplier of fabricated steel products in northern Ontario with Jim's youngest son, Terry, at the helm. Terry's older brother, the late Dick Nemis, must have admired his high-achieving dad too. In 1983 he named his first mineral exploration company Noront Resources, after Jim's start-up.

Dick Nemis couldn't have guessed it would take almost a quarter century for his company to live up to its namesake.

For years Noront Resources operated, as most junior mining companies do, in relative obscurity: optioning a mineral property here and there, drilling where prospects looked promising, moving on when drilling didn't pan out either because of a lack of economic results, lack of interest from the financiers in Toronto and Vancouver, or both.

The company didn't really start making the mining headlines until Nemis picked up the Windfall Lake gold project in northwestern Quebec in the early aughts. Windfall was his best shot at exploration success before stirrings in the James Bay Lowlands distracted him. Indeed, several years later, Osisko Mining would prove up at least six million ounces of gold there, more than enough to support a "highly profitable new gold mine"[1] that promised to rank in the top ten of Canadian and U.S. gold producers.

In 2003 Nemis, who was drawn to treasure hunts like a wasp to Chardonnay, decided to roll the dice on Neil Novak's shiny new base-metals discovery in the James Bay Lowlands. And in 2007 Noront finally made its big hit: the Eagle's Nest nickel-copper-platinum group metals deposit that ignited the Ring of Fire.

Just before the ceremony in June 2008 when Nemis received the TSX Venture 50 Top Mining Company award for his company's spectacular share price performance, a representative from the investor relations firm Agoracom interviewed Nemis outside the stock exchange. Nemis explained in a confident, persuasive tone, "It certainly is without a doubt the biggest staking rush in the last 40 or 50 years in Canada. The ministry can't keep up with registering the claims . . . this is [a] huge play. People have to realize that this year alone there will probably be 60 to 100 million dollars being spent in the area. There is nowhere in Canada that is going to see that kind of exploration work. None. . . . This is something special, something people should keep their eye on and keep the faith of course."

A month later, Noront discovered the Blackbird chromite deposit less than one kilometre from the Eagle's Nest nickel-copper discovery. The chromite discovery was another important milestone for Noront because it diversified the company's commodity portfolio and proved there was more than one major deposit on Noront's ground in the Ring of Fire. The new find also marked the beginning of Noront's practice of naming every significant discovery after a bird native to Canada's boreal forest.

But the coup by Rosseau Asset Management in October 2008 put an abrupt end to the Nemis era, taking much of the fun and excitement surrounding the Ring of Fire play with it.

✳

Rosseau insiders Joseph Hamilton and Paul Parisotto took the helm as interim co-CEOs. In June 2009, they found a permanent CEO, Wes Hanson, to fill the role. Hanson had come from the gold side of the industry, once serving as a vice-president of technical services for international gold producer Kinross Gold. He was seen as a good fit for Noront's ambitions because of his experience developing mines and managing community relations in remote locations.

The new management considered the Windfall gold property in Quebec a distraction and quickly sold it off to another junior, Eagle Hill Exploration. It was a colossal misjudgment. Current owner Osisko Mining expects the Windfall deposit to generate at least C$8 billion in revenue over an eighteen-year mine life starting in 2024.

Noront geologists suspected there was gold in the Ring of Fire too. But it was a bear to find. "It's a challenging area to work in not just because of the lack of outcrop [rock that penetrates surface cover] but because when you are interpreting structure from magnetics, you can come up with some great interpretations in two dimensions, but interpreting that third dimension is difficult," said Noront vice-president of exploration Ryan Weston in an online presentation in 2021.[2]

Instead, Noront stumbled upon the gold in 2009 when the exploration team was drilling for more nickel at Eagle Two, the discovery that had given Bill White his hole in one. Along with nickel, the drillers simultaneously intersected gold mineralization within a major fault zone. Noront named the newly discovered gold zone Triple J after the discovery team (Jeremy Niemi, Jim Atkinson, and Joanne Jobin), but quietly put the resulting data on the shelf while they focused on chromium and nickel.

Hanson's first job as CEO was to consolidate the growing resources of chromite in the Ring of Fire. But Noront, as previously described, failed in its bid to take over Freewest and its chromite assets in the region. Given the choice between shares in a speculative play with no guarantee of success, or a cash payout from Cliffs, Freewest shareholders naturally chose the latter.

The following year, China, always on the hunt for new resources to supply the country's massive infrastructure projects, started circling the Ring of Fire. In May 2011, the state-owned steel company Baosteel inked a US$17.7 million deal to buy a 9.9 percent share in Noront with the option to increase its holding to 19.9 percent. Yuanqing Xu, head of the Americas region for Baosteel Resources International, joined the Noront board, later to be replaced by Bo Liu, senior manager of Baosteel's global resources development.

By that time Nemis, never one to give up, had re-emerged as chairman of Bold Ventures, a new company established to investigate geophysical anomalies west of the Ring of Fire on the premise that the favourable geology for metals stretched to the Manitoba border, at least. He was his usual understated self when asked who might finance a road or railroad that would connect the expanding mineral resources to markets, the Ring of Fire's missing link: "It could be a big Chinese company that comes in and takes over Cliffs, because $2 billion for some of these guys is chicken feed."[3]

The market knew better. After recovering somewhat following the Rosseau intervention, Noront's share price resumed its slide on Toronto's venture exchange, finally dipping below 50 cents in September 2011 and never really recovering. Investors were acutely aware that without a firm commitment from either the public or private sector to build a transport corridor to the region, and at least a partial buy-in from the First Nations in the region, there could be no mine.

"If the financiers in downtown Toronto see any kind of risk, they move on to the next thing," Nemis told *Sudbury Mining Solutions Journal*.[4] "They're looking at [the Ring of Fire] and saying, 'We love the Hudson Bay Lowlands and we think there's going to be all kinds of things found in the future, but we don't know when that's going to happen, so our money is going to go to shorter term opportunities.' When there is some clarity on the issue of infrastructure, everything up there will boom."

But enough investors were keeping the faith to allow Noront to stay afloat. Resource Capital Funds, a multinational mining investment firm, gave Noront C$10 million in May 2012 in exchange for almost 20 million shares. The private placement was enough to fund a drilling campaign to build resources at the Eagle's Nest nickel-copper-PGE deposit, the first Noront intended to place into production.

By September Noront had completed a feasibility study outlining a 20 million tonne nickel-copper deposit averaging 1.1–1.7 percent nickel and about 1 percent copper, plus platinum and palladium credits at Eagle's Nest, pretty decent by global standards. The study estimated it would cost about US$609 million to build a mine that would last eleven years.

Meanwhile, Noront was trying hard to improve relations with the First Nations in the area, forming its own alliances outside of any government interference. The company recognized that early dialogue and consultation with communities in the region was key to its survival.

Leading that drive was chief operating officer Paul Semple, a mining engineer by training. According to those who knew him, Semple became the heart and soul of Noront, winning respect from First Nations in the area and creating a culture of inclusion.

Semple would not tolerate racism in the ranks. Geologist Matt Downey recalls the COO moving swiftly when rumours of anti-Indigenous sentiment reached head office from Noront's Esker camp in the Ring of Fire. Noront ran its exploration program from Esker, but the camp itself was owned and operated by a contractor. Semple arranged for Noront to buy the camp so that it had better control over the culture there.

The COO strengthened ties with the First Nations by encouraging Hanson to hire Glenn Nolan, former chief of the Missanabie Cree First Nation, as vice-president of Aboriginal affairs. Nolan is a past president of the Prospectors & Developers Association of Canada, the first Indigenous president in the organization's history.

Semple wanted to set an example for the world about how industry-Indigenous partnerships should work. On an April 2012 visit to Nibinamik First Nation, a tiny community due west of the Ring of Fire, he said: "We believe there is an opportunity right now for industry and First Nations to develop a world-class model of how we can work together. Our goal is to set the standard, to supersede the current industry standard in how we work with Aboriginal people."[5]

Under Semple's leadership, Noront established a sustainability department, practically unheard of in the junior mining sector at the time. To encourage Indigenous participation in the workforce, the company became a partner in Nishnawbe Education and Training, a program that prepares locals for employment in mining by providing skills-based training and career guidance.

"Paul was a big guy with a big presence, but he was really nice and soft at heart," recalled Downey, who, when I spoke to him in 2020, had worked as a geologist for Noront for a dozen years. "He had this ability to bring people together and to really kickstart things. We made a lot of progress because of him."

By 2020 a majority of the workforce at the company's Esker camp self-identified as Indigenous. Two of the First Nations in the Matawa Tribal Council, Marten Falls and Aroland, had become equity shareholders in Noront. The company was holding regular community town halls in English and Oji-Cree and supplying all of its written communication in Oji-Cree, Cree, English, and French.

As part of this process, Noront received constant feedback from the communities. Many of them said they supported development but were worried about tailings dam failures, polluted water discharge, ugly scars on the landscape, and waste rock piles. As a result of these concerns, Noront went back to the drawing board to redesign the Eagle's Nest mine. The proposed open pit was scrapped in favour of an underground mine that would have a much smaller environmental footprint. To eliminate waste rock piles and the risk of dam failure, the engineers came up with an innovative way to store waste materials produced by the concentrator — potentially toxic when they are exposed to the elements — underground. Processing water would be recycled instead of released.

Semple persevered through these challenging times, but as the share price continued its slide, Wes Hanson's days became numbered. In January 2013, the same year Ontario entered negotiations with Indigenous groups to find a way to develop the Ring of Fire, Hanson resigned as president and chief executive officer. Once again, Paul

Parisotto stepped in as interim president and CEO until a replacement could be found.

That replacement was Alan Coutts. Coutts is what people in the business world would call a straight shooter. The veteran geologist is always impeccably groomed, his white moustache and beard neatly trimmed. He is rarely seen in public without a well-fitting suit and tie. Elegant, clear, and precise, he is the antithesis of the bushy-faced, plaid-shirted, beer-swilling geotype.

Coutts had come full circle. Well before the Ring of Fire discovery, he had been working as a geologist for Falconbridge, one of Canada's top mining companies, the same company whose president had filled young Neil Novak's head with stories of global prospecting so many years earlier. When Falconbridge was swallowed up in 2006 by Xstrata, a massive firm headquartered in Switzerland, Coutts was assigned to the multinational's nickel division.

"We were busy doing a lot of a mergers and acquisitions and by 2008, the discovery by Noront Resources had caught our attention because it was an interesting high-grade nickel-copper deposit," said Coutts. Xstrata had inherited a Sudbury nickel-copper smelter with the Falconbridge purchase and was looking for ore to feed the ravenous beast. Eagle's Nest looked like the perfect source.

Xstrata did some due diligence on Eagle's Nest and decided against investing in the end because the project was too grassroots, too risky for a big company like Xstrata to pursue. And likely far too remote. Instead, the Anglo-Swiss company purchased a more advanced nickel asset in Australia called Jubilee.

Coutts was transferred to Perth to run the Jubilee operations, but as he told me later, he "always remembered the Ring of Fire, the quality of that deposit and the exploration upside in the area."

In May 2013 — the same year Cliffs pulled its hat from the Ring — Xstrata was purchased by Glencore, another global mining powerhouse. Coutts again found himself at an uncertain juncture in his career. Out of the blue, he got a call from Tom Anselmi, a Noront board member who went on to become COO of the Edmonton Oilers hockey team, suggesting he come back to Canada to lead Noront and advance its prospects in the Ring of Fire.

He jumped at the chance. "You get to a point in your career when you want to do something that has value and that you think is important," he told me in 2020, seven years into his job. "This project is an important part of the economic and social fabric of Ontario and Canada. We want to be part of the success story and be the group that opens this area up collaboratively with government and First Nations partners."

Coutts was equally proud of, and wanted to preserve, the accomplished management and board of directors the junior company had managed to assemble. By 2020 the team boasted Glencore's former VP of Projects & Exploration Stephen Flewelling; Harry Winston Inc.'s former VP of Internal Audit and Business Development Greg Rieveley; Cliffs' former senior geologist Ryan Weston; Seneca Engineering's former VP Mark Baker; and Nolan, the former First Nations chief and PDAC president. In 2017, the past president and CEO of the Canadian Council for Aboriginal Business, JP Gladu, joined them. If anyone had any doubt about the quality of the Ring of Fire deposits, they need look no further than the reputations of the Noront team.

Coutts adopted Semple's model of community consultation while trying to move the project along at a pace faster than molasses. By May 2014, Noront had received provincial approval to mine the Eagle's Nest nickel-copper and Blackbird chromite deposits for a period of twenty-one years, subject to certain requirements of the Ontario Mining Act.

The year 2015 was pivotal for the company. Franco-Nevada, a gold royalty firm with deep pockets, loaned Noront US$25 million to purchase all the assets Cliffs had abandoned in the Ring of Fire. The final purchase price was C$20 million, a steal compared to the hundreds of millions Cliffs spent during the four years it was active there. The purchase consolidated all the major discoveries in the Ring of Fire and made Noront by far the largest claimholder in the camp. And in a nod to Noront's efforts to address First Nations concerns in the region, the junior won the Environmental and Social Responsibility Award bestowed annually by the Prospectors & Developers Association of Canada. Alas, the award turned out to be bittersweet. Semple, who had spearheaded the company's sustainability program, died suddenly from complications of kidney disease in April 2015, just one month after the awards ceremony.

With the new infusion of cash into the Ring of Fire, KWG CEO Frank Smeenk revived his own efforts to attract more investment to the play. In 2016, he released a video of bikini-clad young women frolicking in the summer sun to promote the area's metal deposits. "Sex sells," Smeenk explained when journalists asked why he would do such a thing.

Smeenk might have hoped a clip featuring young models shaking their rears while discussing the merits of the Ring of Fire metal deposits would go viral. Maybe it would draw attention to the region that, until this time, had all but disappeared from general public discourse. But the video could not have been more tone-deaf. Predictably, the marketing stunt was met with a combination of ridicule and indignation. And it made the mining industry seem even more the misogynist boys' club it was already perceived to be. Women in the sector flipped a collective bird at Smeenk and carried on with their work.

Noront made another major discovery in September 2017, this time a volcanogenic massive sulphide deposit rich in copper and zinc. By 2020, Noront had identified ten such copper-zinc lenses, of which three are together known as the Nikka deposit ("Canada Goose" in Oji-Cree). Noront aimed to prove there was a minimum of 5 to 10 million tonnes of copper-zinc ore at Nikka to feed a future milling operation.

And in 2018, with an improved understanding of the region's gold potential, coupled with rising gold prices, Noront revived its gold exploration program with the intent of spinning off the resulting finds or finding a partner to develop them. But the challenge of exploring for the precious metal in the wetlands lingered. Weston decided to try soil sampling, a well-developed exploration technique in areas with an established soil profile, but less frequently applied in swampy areas. To test the technique, he ran a soil sampling survey over the Triple J gold zone discovered in 2009 to see if the samples could identify the deposit as an anomaly. They did. Now Noront had yet another valuable commodity to investigate using a proven technique. A separate company, privately owned Juno Corp. led by financier Robert Cudney from the Cyrano's trio, was equally inspired to explore for the precious metal in the northern half of the camp and, as of 2022, continued to hold much of the ground there.

In 2019, Noront took a step further by choosing the northern city of Sault Ste. Marie for a C$1 billion ferrochrome smelter the company hoped to build to process the Ring of Fire's chromite resources. Four cities, including the Sault, Sudbury, Thunder Bay, and Timmins, had been vying for the jobs and economic shot in the arm the plant could provide.

"In the end we were persuaded to go with Sault Ste. Marie because it is located on the Great Lakes and offers a lower long-term operating cost advantage," Coutts said in a May 2019 press release.

But the chosen city was divided. A few months after the Sault won the competition, a group of physicians wrote a letter suggesting there could be an exodus of medical professionals from the town if the plant were built. They worried about the potential of the plant to emit toxins. The letter sparked opposition to the smelter from thousands of residents of the economically depressed city who feared for their future health. Some even conjured the fate of Hinkley, California, the town in the movie *Erin Brockovich*, which dramatized a legal fight against a utility company that allowed chromium-tainted water to leak from its wastewater holding ponds, poisoning Hinkley's residents.[6]

Nevertheless, Noront moved forward with planning. In September 2019, the company signed agreements with Algoma Steel Inc. and engineering firm Hatch Ltd. to facilitate mine development and build the processing facilities. Algoma awarded Noront an option to lease one of its brownfield properties in the Sault for a period of 99 years. Hatch would perform engineering and provide project support for the Ring of Fire chromite and Eagle's Nest projects.

❋

But just as the Ring of Fire appeared to be progressing again, Richard Nemis's health started to wane. The first indication that something was amiss was a lump on his wrist. According to his sister Melody, he fought hard and thought he would recover, but in March 2019 — as one of his favourite events, the PDAC convention, was winding down — cancer took his life. Before his death, Nemis told his daughter Jennifer to use his name to "do some good." To honour that wish, his family started the Richard Nemis Ring of Fire First Nations Community Trust.

"It was really important for my father to take care of people," Jennifer told me. "He was concerned about some of the issues in the North, like clean running water and lack of supplies. This is a way to honour him by hopefully raising some funds and giving the people of the North some reassurance that we're all trying to work together on this project."

Among those who offered online condolences, Edmund Elbert spoke for many: "[Richard was] one of the key people that gave me an interest in the mining industry. [I] will miss his positive attitude. He was never a quitter whether it be for his companies or for fighting his sickness. I have always looked up to Dick and will forever hold high respect for him."

With help from the Ontario government, Noront further strengthened bonds with First Nations communities that aspired to build infrastructure in the region. Under established protocol, mining companies are responsible for the environmental assessments for both the mine they want to build and the roads leading to the mine. But Indigenous people near the Ring of Fire knew the land better than anyone and wanted to play a lead role in the permitting process. In an unprecedented arrangement, the province agreed to fund Webequie and Marten Falls to complete environmental assessments on the legs of the road leading to their communities, despite objections by the nearby communities of Neskantaga and Eabametoong.

Noront, a company held together by periodic cash infusions and determination, continued to explore. The strategy was to build a pipeline of deposits that could be developed after the Eagle's Nest nickel-copper-PGE deposit went into production in 2028. Some of this expensive work was funded by a tax relief mechanism called flow-through financing. The scheme encourages mineral exploration by allowing companies to pass on tax credits for exploration to their shareholders.[7]

But Noront was caught in a precarious position. When the company had raised C$26 million in February 2008, it had just over 100 million shares outstanding. That shareholding quadrupled to more than 400 million shares by the end of 2020 because of the successive financings Noront had to complete in order to keep the lights on, each one dumping more shares on the market and diluting the value of those held by existing shareholders. Plus, there were the huge loans from Resource Capital and Franco-Nevada to be repaid.

In 2021 a coalition consisting of MiningWatch Canada, Greenpeace Canada, Osgoode Hall Law School's Environmental Justice and Sustainability Clinic, and the Council of Canadians called on the Ontario Securities

Commission to investigate Noront for its failure to disclose the "significant" First Nations opposition in the area to mine development on Indigenous traditional lands, arguing that Noront was deceiving investors into thinking the company could proceed with a mine unimpeded.

By that point Noront's share price had been floundering in the 10–20 cent per share range for months. Cash, as always, was limited. The original payback dates for loans had long since expired.

Time was running out for the Little Junior That Could.

✳

Coutts hoped Noront would get a boost from a new cornerstone investor, Australia's Wyloo Metals. In December 2020, Wyloo agreed to acquire the roughly 96 million shares, US$15 million in debt, and 1 percent royalty in Eagle's Nest production held by Resource Capital Funds.

Wyloo is the mining division of Tattarang, one of Australia's largest private investment groups. The group is headed by Andrew "Twiggy" Forrest, one of the wealthiest men in the world, who made his fortune building Fortescue Metals Group to mine and ship iron ore from Australia to China. Forrest's stated ambition, on the cusp of his sixtieth birthday, was to establish a green energy powerhouse in Australia. He framed the Noront deal as part of a broader strategy to develop critical commodities required to decarbonize the global economy.

Inevitably, as a result of the competitive nature of the sector and a worldwide scarcity of high-quality metal deposits, other sharks awoke to the opportunity to control one of Canada's best stores of undeveloped critical minerals on the cheap. They began to circle. The Ring of Fire's nickel, a key ingredient in EV lithium-ion batteries, was especially desirable. Demand for the metal was expected to surge by more than 500 percent from 2020 to 2030.[8]

In April 2021, the biggest mining company in the world, BHP, approached Noront with an offer to acquire a 9.9 percent stake in the junior. Noront management was keen to acquiesce, but their new cornerstone investor Wyloo refused to consent to the deal. BHP, which had recently inked an agreement with Tesla to supply nickel for the carmaker's EV batteries, tried again a month later with a new offer to acquire 19.9

percent of Noront at a 10 percent premium to the market price, worth about 25 cents per share at the time. Wyloo still wouldn't budge.

As many suspected, Wyloo had loftier ambitions than just being Noront's largest share and debt holder. In June 2021, the company announced its intention to make an unsolicited bid for the remaining shares of Noront priced at 31.5 cents per share, putting a value of C$133 million on the junior. If the deal proved successful, the board of directors of the new Noront would be led by none other than Twiggy himself. Forrest intended to replicate in Canada's Ring of Fire the success he'd had in Western Australia, where he transformed junior Fortescue into a A$65 billion mining giant.

Fortescue had recently inked a half-billion-dollar joint venture with Indigenous titleholders to co-manage the development of new mines in the Pilbara iron ore district of Australia. Forrest argued that creating competitive Indigenous-owned businesses and genuine employment opportunities for Indigenous people trumped the mining sector's traditional practice of "buying your access with vapid buckets of cash."[9]

Could Forrest negotiate a similar deal with the First Nations in the Ring of Fire region? He hoped a personal letter to the Matawa Tribal Chiefs might help:

> Ever since I was a baby, my childhood involved growing up with Indigenous children and being raised as a tribe like one big village, by their parents as well as my own. I grew up speaking the language of the [Yamatji] Aboriginal people, and they were my brothers and sisters. I am no longer a child, but I am an adult who has never forgotten the friends and families of my youth, and I have ensured that the largest part of our team, of our entire workforce, is our Indigenous Australians . . . until we meet in person, please accept a big hug from me.[10]

The Noront board immediately adopted a "poison pill" strategy, a legal manoeuvre companies use to prevent creeping takeovers by making shares prohibitively expensive to buy on the open market.

But despite Coutts's desire to personally see the Ring of Fire through to development, Wyloo's takeover bid effectively put Noront "in play." The expectation in the investment community was that another offer would come along to spark a bidding war. Sure enough, in July 2021 BHP offered to acquire Noront outright for 55 cents per share. Coutts lost control of the narrative.

The Noront board again encouraged shareholders to tender their shares to the BHP offer. But again, Wyloo threw a wrench in the works by refusing to cooperate. The company's management accused Noront of stymying Wyloo's plans by not providing the technical information required to make a counter-offer. In September, Wyloo converted its US$15 million convertible loan into common shares of Noront, increasing its equity stake to about 37.3 percent from 24.2 percent and giving the private Australian company even more leverage to fend off BHP.

Australia's second-wealthiest man, with a personal net worth of roughly A$27 billion in 2021, pitted against the world's largest mining company? With such enormous egos at stake, the stage was set for a protracted corporate pissing match.

Territory marking carried on through the fall of 2021. BHP raised its bid to 75 cents per share in cash, a 36 percent premium over its previous offer, putting a value on Noront of C$419 million. But BHP needed at least 50 percent of shares it didn't already own to be tendered to the offer for their takeover to succeed. Shareholders, some of whom had held onto their shares since those heady days post-discovery, scoffed at what some considered corporate theft. BHP extended its tender deadline three times, but still some shareholders wouldn't budge. The company finally called "uncle" and agreed to sit down with Wyloo to hammer out an arrangement that would be satisfactory to all.

But that strategy didn't work either. The talks failed.

"We both tried to get to a transaction that fully reflected the value of the assets, but unfortunately, we couldn't get there together," said Luca Giacovazzi, the head of Wyloo Metals.[11] "We've got a view on the value of these assets and if we don't think BHP is going to pay that price, we're not going to sell it."

In mid-December — six months after its initial run at Noront — Wyloo offered $1.10 per share in a deal that would give shareholders the choice to continue to participate in the growth potential of Noront, or sell out for cash. The offer sent Noront shares skyrocketing 52 percent to C$1.11 a share, the highest they'd been in over a decade. How quickly the value of the Little Junior That Could had jumped, from just C$133 million in mid-2021 to C$617 million! Noront's board of directors and shareholders started to warm to the deal, though even Giacovazzi considered the junior undervalued at that price.

"It blows my mind that people think it's a big price," Giacovazzi told the *Australian Mining Review*.[12] "When you look at something like Chalice [a nickel deposit in Australia], this thing's got three times the grade of Chalice with a huge number of tonnes already drilled out. It's a no-brainer for us."

On December 22, 2021, Noront and Wyloo announced they had entered into a binding agreement that would see Wyloo acquire up to all of the outstanding common shares of Noront it did not already own. BHP dropped out of the race in exchange for a kill fee of C$17.8 million, saying the company did not see "adequate long-term value" in raising its 75-cents-per-share bid any higher.

Noront shareholders were given the option of retaining their shares in a new Noront whose board of directors would be led by Andrew Forrest. But enough tendered shares to the cash offer that Wyloo was able to complete a full acquisition. In March 2022, Giacovazzi flew to Thunder Bay to meet with business owners, politicians, and First Nations leaders to relay his vision for the Eagle's Nest project.

By April 7, the deal was done. Wyloo stated in a coincident press release that it would adhere to four key commitments: to develop Eagle's Nest as a net zero emissions mine; to spend C$25 million on feasibility studies to investigate the potential for battery material production in Ontario; to set a target of C$100 million in contracts to Indigenous-led businesses; and to create and sustain Indigenous and northern Ontario employment opportunities. Wyloo later changed Noront's name to Ring of Fire Metals "to reflect the unique culture of the organization, while also paying homage to its Canadian roots and the region's history."

Though Wyloo said it is "committing to transform the Eagle's Nest nickel deposit into the new international standard for responsible mining practices," stakeholders in the Ring of Fire may be in the dark about the company's activities going forward. Whereas Noront was required to report to securities regulators and shareholders on a regular basis, Wyloo is a private company and, as such, is not required to issue public statements about its activities.

PART II

People and the Planet

CHAPTER 6

Whose Land? Our Land

In October 2020, Monique Edwards and James Kataquapit launched a canoe into the mouth of the Attawapiskat River. The middle-aged Cree couple was about to embark on a fifteen-day voyage upriver from the west coast of James Bay into the interior of Ontario's Far North.

Their mission? To send a message to politicians and the mining industry: we're here and we're watching. Their destination? The confluence of the Mukutei and Attawapiskat Rivers, where mineral deposits lie hidden beneath slow-flowing waters. Esker camp, headquarters for Noront's and now Wyloo's exploration team, is perched on a gravel ridge just east of the Mukutei on the highest ground in the area. During peak exploration season, a crew of up to seventy mostly Indigenous people work at the fly-in camp, living in canvas platform tents connected by a raised boardwalk that keeps their feet and equipment dry.

The area is as remote as it gets, but if provincial road planning to the communities near the Ring of Fire succeeds, mines will likely follow, starting with the Eagle's Nest nickel-copper-PGE underground operation in 2028. There is enough chromium, copper, gold, nickel, and zinc underlying the swamp to sustain operations for decades, perhaps even centuries.

Along their 222-kilometre journey, James and Monique passed tree-topped limestone islands rising out of the river like birthday cakes, remnants of a reef formed in an ancient sea. A little further along, they canoed past remains of a different kind: the ghost of the open-pit

Victor mine, where De Beers extracted hundreds of thousands of some of the world's most valuable diamonds for eleven years. The only other evidence of human habitation was the greying wooden crosses marking the gravesites of their elders, a couple of fly-in fishing camps, and some detritus left over from the mineral exploration rush of 2007 or wilderness canoeists. There were few dwellings, no roads, hardly a soul in sight.

You might guess that no one cares, or feels responsible, for the land.

James and Monique intended to dispel that notion. Like others in the coastal community of Attawapiskat First Nation, home to about 1,500 residents, they spend a lot of time on the land and appreciate its bounty. They want to preserve the flora, fauna, and waterways for future generations. It's their way of honouring the seventh generation principle, which insists all decisions must consider the impacts on community members seven generations into the future.

They figured the best way to do that would be to mark what they considered their territory. They cut wooden poles and attached colourful flags to them. They erected the poles where miners and politicians might see them. One of the largest of the colourful displays read:

> We are people at risk at the end of the Attawapiskat River. This water flows into [Weeneebayko] territory. All rivers flow down. Mukutei River connects to Attawapiskat River and ends at our traditional lands. It is our responsibility to protect our survival and our way of life. Our children, grandchildren, great grandchildren and generations to come depend on us. Everyone matters, including us.

The video of their journey garnered eighty-nine shares on Facebook in the weeks after their return. James and Monique repeated the trip the following year, arriving at the same destination on October 13, 2021. This time, they invited others to join them, bearing their own family flags to attach to more meegwum poles along the river "to show this land is not vacant."

They represent the guardians of Yehewin Aski, the Breathing Lands. The region is home to several thousand mostly First Nations people who generally speak Oji-Cree in the interior and the Swampy Cree dialect along the coast of James Bay. Some of the communities support mining development with conditions. Others do not.

There are two tribal councils involved in the decision-making. The Matawa Tribal Council consists of the nine Cree, Ojibway, and Oji-Cree communities closest to the Ring of Fire, including four in the south accessible by all-season roads (Aroland, Constance Lake, Ginoogaming, and Long Lake) and five further north accessible only by winter road and air (Eabametoong, Marten Falls, Neskantaga, Nibinamik, and Webequie). The Mushkegowuk Council based in Moose Factory represents a total of seven Cree First Nations. Four lie along the James Bay coast a few hundred kilometres downstream of the Ring of Fire: Attawapiskat, Fort Albany, Kashechewan, and Moose Cree. They are connected by a 310-kilometre winter road they work together to maintain.

Most of the Nations in the region fall under Treaty 9. The treaty was spawned in the summer of 1901, when some Nations requested action from the Canadian government to stem the flow of non-Indigenous trappers and prospectors on their traditional lands and halt the decline of the local beaver population. When government commissioners paddled and portaged their way to the area to negotiate, they offered the Nations the right to continue hunting and fishing for sustenance and trade, along with an annual stipend from the government. In exchange, the white men would be allowed to lay down railway tracks, dig mines, cut trees, and establish their own settlements within the treaty area.

In 1905–06, Treaty 9 became law, one of eleven post-Confederation numbered treaties negotiated with Indigenous peoples in Canada between 1871 and 1921. The Indigenous signatories had to forever "cede, release, surrender and yield up . . . all their rights, titles, and privileges" to lands within the treaty limits to the Crown.[1] Each chief received a copy of the document. And a Union Jack flag to wave in the wilderness. Treaty annuities were set at C$4 per person.

While Treaty 9 represents a surrendering of Indigenous sovereignty to the Canadian government in the written document, descendants of the Indigenous signatories believe the original, orally expressed intention to *share* the land and its resources is closer to the truth. Historian and educator John Long agrees. According to the surviving commissioners' journals, there is a chasm between what was explained to the First

Nations and what the treaty document says.[2] He argues that the Nations were anticipating a more equitable co-existence along the lines of the fur-trading model they were accustomed to.

But there was no sharing, only plundering.

✳

At roughly the same time James and Monique were motoring upriver, two residents of Neskantaga, an interior fly-in community of about 300 at the headwaters of the Attawapiskat, travelled south to Toronto. They staged a sit-in on the manicured lawns of the Ontario legislature to protest the water crisis in their community.

Neskantaga, whose chief Chris Moonias opposed road development to the remote Ring of Fire, had been under a boil-water advisory for more than a quarter of a century. Just before the sit-in during the pandemic, community members were evacuated to hotels in Thunder Bay because of the latest contamination: an oily substance in the water reservoir.

It is difficult to run a community or build much-needed housing, much less contribute to mine and land use planning, when the water running from your taps is undrinkable. Back in 2016, the Trudeau government pledged to fix the water treatment problems in all Indigenous communities by March 2021. The feds threw millions of dollars at the problem, but they did not meet their deadline.

Grand Chief Alvin Fiddler of Nishnawbe Aski Nation, representing forty-nine communities in northern Ontario, including Neskantaga, issued a statement during the sit-in:

> Canada is known as one of the greatest countries in the world to live in, but the people of Neskantaga are being denied the basic human right of access to clean water. Treaty No. 9 and Treaty No. 5 represent the nation-to-nation relationship between the people of Nishnawbe Aski and the Crown. We fully support Chief Moonias, and we look to the governments of Ontario and Canada to honour the treaties and provide the necessities of life to the people of Neskantaga.

Chief Moonias was smart to raise a little hell about his community's prolonged boil-water advisory. His outcry forced government officials keen to get the Ring of Fire development and its tax revenues moving to pay attention to the communities in the region and their struggles with not only clean water but social problems and housing. In July 2021, Ottawa finally pledged nearly C$8 billion to settle class-action lawsuits spearheaded by three First Nations, including Neskantaga, over unsafe drinking water and to fix water-quality problems in communities across Canada. The agreement provided C$1.5 billion in compensation for roughly 142,000 people in communities that have posted drinking-water advisories over the years, and another C$400 million for a First Nation Economic and Cultural Restoration Fund.

But Moonias was also walking a tightrope with his objection to road development to the region. If he were too passive, the soul-crushing social and infrastructure problems in his community could carry on indefinitely and even worsen if the road became a route for more drugs and alcohol to enter the region. But by vowing to block the road construction, he blocks the very means by which his community's water treatment plant might be properly maintained and regularly serviced.

"The promise of sustainable clean, drinkable water remains theoretical," wrote Ryan Moore in the *Toronto Star*.[3] "A lack of infrastructure — from roads to equipment — has undermined construction projects. . . . Lack of roads, in particular, means many infrastructure projects, including water treatment plants, are delayed, incomplete or go unrepaired for great lengths of time."

Chris Moonias stepped down as chief in 2021 and was replaced by Wayne Moonias. But he remained defiant on behalf of his community. On November 25, 2021, Neskantaga launched a legal challenge against the Ontario government to oppose "reckless mining development in the Ring of Fire," accusing the province of failing to fulfill its duty to consult and accommodate by making it difficult for Neskantaga to participate in consultation during the COVID-19 pandemic. Moonias tweeted: "I live on the Attawapiskat River where the proposed so-called Ring of Fire is. There has not been any consultation. We will not let them cross our river."

In a new and bitter twist to a decade-long battle, Neskantaga named not only the Ontario government in the lawsuit but their Ojibway neighbour and fellow tribal council member Marten Falls, the proponent of a community access road that would run through Neskantaga territory and connect with the proposed Northern Road Link to the Ring of Fire.

✳

In the early hours of Sunday, April 10, 2016, seven children were rushed to the Attawaspiskat hospital with possible drug overdoses. The kids, some as young as seven, were showing symptoms resembling those of recent suicide attempts in the community. Over the past forty-eight hours, there had been sixteen suspected suicide attempts. The community of Attawapiskat declared a state of emergency.[4] Hundreds of suicides and attempted suicides had been reported in the community over the last couple of years. The crisis had been brewing for decades, some would say at least a century.

First came the Indian Act of 1876, the primary legislation governing how the Government of Canada interacts with the more than 600 Indigenous bands and their members in the country. Its intent was to take many different Indigenous cultures, generalize them, and then assimilate them into non-Indigenous society, to make them well-behaved citizens of the British Empire. The act imposed elections of chiefs and councils, who act on behalf of the federal government. Described as an "evolving, para-doxical document that has enabled trauma, human rights violations, and social and cultural disruption for generations of Indigenous peoples,"[5] the act has been amended several times over the past century.

"The Indian Act is actually a study in contradictions," writes Bob Joseph in his book *Indigenous Relations*.[6] "Its purpose was to assimi-late, but in practice it segregated and marginalized Aboriginal Peoples; restricted their ability to be part of the local economy; forced children to attend separate schools, often far away from their families; outlawed their traditions, languages and culture; and restricted their ability to mingle with mainstream Euro-settlers."

Initially, the Attawapiskat Cree largely escaped the worst of the Indian Act's abominations. They remained semi-nomadic hunters, trappers, and fishers who lived along James Bay's northwestern shores and within its river systems, including the bountiful Attawapiskat River. But when they were brought under Treaty 9 in 1930, the Canadian government insisted they send their children to residential schools or forfeit their family allowance payment. The arrangement stifled their semi-nomadic lifestyle by creating a permanent settlement supported by federal dollars, a mini welfare state. Many people ceased venturing into the wilderness except, perhaps, to supplement their meagre, expensive diets with fish and game.

The housing erected to establish the permanent community was of the cheapest quality, unable to withstand the harsh conditions of Canada's north. A 2013 audit by Canada's Aboriginal and Northern Affairs department revealed that of the 316 homes in Attawapiskat, 85 percent were unfit for human habitation,[7] the result of overcrowding, flooding, and poor construction. Furthermore, under the terms of the Indian Act, reserve land was "held and administered by His Majesty, for the benefit of the Indians": a seemingly innocuous clause that in fact stripped residents of their ability to borrow funds to build a house or start a business, a vital stepping stone to prosperity for so many Canadians. A lack of clean drinking water exacerbated the misery.

The Canadian government's attempts to absorb Indigenous peoples into its largely Eurocentric culture by forcing children to board at schools funded by the government and run by the churches left a particularly indelible mark. According to the 2015 Truth and Reconciliation Commission (TRC), the odds of children dying at these residential schools was 1 in 25, about the same as for Canadian infantry soldiers in World War II. Indeed, the use of ground-penetrating radar helped detect hundreds of their potential unmarked graves across the country, forcing Canadians to acknowledge this legacy of horror and accelerate attempts at reconciliation. Not just "cultural genocide" as the TRC reported, but genocide plain and simple.

Those who did survive were stripped of their language and culture. The custodians of residential schools often emotionally, physically, and sexually abused the children under their care. Of all the horrific incidents that took place at these residential schools during the twentieth century, some of the worst were inflicted on Attawapiskat's children. The Canadian government rounded them up and sent them to St. Anne's school in Fort Albany, a prison-like hellscape that allegedly boasted its own homemade electric chair to punish the children. In 1992, in a series of interviews conducted by the Ontario Provincial Police, survivors relayed stories of rape, torture, and other trauma that took place at St. Anne's from 1941 to 1972.

According to mental health experts,[8] this level of abuse is not something you get over. Rather it gets passed down through generations. In some cases, parents, grandparents, and great-grandparents all suffered at the hands of the St. Anne's monsters, who became their caregiving role models.

Is it any wonder that today's youth are so despairing?

✳

Shortly after the concurrent protests against the Ring of Fire infrastructure development by Attawapiskat and Neskantaga, communities at either end of the Attawapiskat River that connects them, I put a call in to Brandyn Chum, a thirty-three-year-old Oji-Cree living in Thunder Bay. He is less concerned about mining's impact on the land than about securing a career. He started working at Noront's Esker camp east of the Mukutei River doing odd jobs when he was twenty-one. He says the company has been good to him, giving him increasing amounts of responsibility, including maintaining the camp's water treatment plant.

Chum has moved around a lot in his life. He is a member of the Moose Cree First Nation, based in Moose Factory at the south end of James Bay, but grew up in Kapuskasing and Toronto before moving to Thunder Bay for high school. He graduated in 2006, enrolling in film school and training as a laboratory assistant before moving back in with his mom and stepdad in Dryden, Ontario. That's when he discovered Noront's Esker camp was looking for help and seized the opportunity to work outdoors and make some decent money.

Chum says he wouldn't want to live in the lowlands, even though that's where his roots lie, if he can avoid it. His dream is to establish a permanent home in Thunder Bay, working on rotation (two weeks on and two weeks off is common) in the Ring of Fire.

"Some of the elders don't want the mine happening. The younger people are for it," he tells me. "I hope I get to be in senior site support up there."

If you journey north from the coastal communities of Moose Factory and Attawapiskat, hugging the curvaceous western shoreline of James and then Hudson Bay, you eventually reach the inlet that leads to the hamlet of Baker Lake in Nunavut. It's the geographic centre of Canada.

Baker Lake has been transformed by gold mining over the past decade. Traditionally, the Inuit community relied on the whims of migrating caribou for sustenance. Some years, residents went hungry. There were few employment opportunities other than government jobs. But since Agnico Eagle Mines opened the Meadowbank gold mine nearby in 2010, two cars have appeared in the driveways of many Inuit homes, for better or worse. Residents have money in the bank.

In 2021 Agnico Eagle earned a spot on *Corporate Knights*' list of the top 100 most sustainable corporations in the world, mainly for the company's efforts at its gold mines on Inuit territory, including Meadowbank, Meliadine, and Amaruq. Agnico is aiming for 100 percent Inuit employment at the mines. Education and training of the local workforce is a big part of that goal. Community development is another, including a pool of funds to support community projects.

So in early 2021 when Agnico purchased the Hope Bay gold project further north, near Cambridge Bay, with the intention of developing yet another gold mine, it drew cheers from the Kivalliq Inuit Association (KIA), which worked with Agnico Eagle to establish and maintain good community relations.

"The KIA recognizes Agnico Eagle Mines as a global leader in the gold mining business and we are excited about what this will mean for all Inuit in Nunavut and especially for our regional counterparts in the Kitikmeot," said the Kivalliq association's president, Kono Tattuinee, in a release.

But not everyone was applauding. The noise and disruption from Agnico's Meadowbank mine drove the caribou away, some say, and hunters must go further afield to access the animals.

"The original proposal was approved in good spirit and trust on our part. We believed that the regulatory system protected our land and wildlife," Joan Scottie, a Baker Lake Inuit resident, wrote in *Nunatsiaq News*.

"However, once the mine went into full operation, we were caught off guard. We didn't expect dust, which now blows and accumulates on the tundra that caribou graze on, to be a serious disturbance to our traditional lifestyle. We also didn't worry that the caribou, which used to be near our community year-round, might be driven away by the disruption from the mine road."

And when the mines run out of ore, will the residents of Baker Lake go hungry again?

"We are unprepared for what's really in store for us," Scottie wrote.

✳

A massive steel structure shaped like a Y dangles from a helicopter. On the steep slope below stands a group of men dressed in orange vests and hardhats. They're looking up, Adam's apples bobbing in their outstretched necks, knees bent for stability.

The wind howling through the mountain pass blows the monstrous steel lattice this way and that, downwash from helicopter blades amplifying its force. The combination of bluster and engine noise is deafening. Even though they wear safety glasses, the men instinctively raise their forearms to their faces to shield their eyes from dust and flying debris.

As the tower — as tall as a six-storey building — comes within reach, the men rush forward as if to form a rugby scrum. They grab hold. For a moment it looks as though they'll be swept skyward like action heroes dangling from the edge of a fleeing jet. But they grip tightly to the rungs of the tower, biceps bulging, bodies swaying to and fro. Together, they manage to wrestle the tower onto an impossibly small pin anchored to the ground. One of them detaches the long line dangling from the helicopter. Their supervisor gives the pilot a double thumbs-up. The chopper whirls away to pick up the next tower for placement along the hydro transmission line.

It's 2012 in the Stikine Valley of northwestern British Columbia, also known as the "Serengeti of North America," territory of the Tahltan Nation. Award-winning filmmaker Nettie Wild is shooting the hydro line construction for *Koneline: Our Land Beautiful*. The line runs 344 kilometres north from Terrace, B.C., into a remote area rich in minerals. It's a scar slicing through a fairy tale mountainscape, a reminder of what we humans sacrifice in the name of the economy and convenience. And it is analogous to the 450 kilometres of new road that would link the Ring of Fire to the Ontario highway network: a "corridor of prosperity" that threatens an untouched wilderness.

Wild's film captures the tug-of-war between conservation and resource development playing out daily on the world stage. As the human population grows and the most accessible natural resources dwindle, the fight is intensifying. And it's moving to ever more remote regions of the globe, often where Indigenous peoples have lived for millennia. The tug-of-war pits the economy against the environment, Indigenous youth against their elders, and rural conservatives against urban liberals. It spares few countries.

But in B.C.'s Stikine Valley, nothing gets done without the approval of the powerful Tahltan Nation. Tahltan territory covers 95,500 square kilometres, about the size of Portugal, or 11 percent of British Columbia plus a sliver of the Yukon. The area includes 5,000 people in two bands: the Tahltan Indian Band, headquartered in Telegraph Creek, and the Iskut First Nation, headquartered in Iskut.

About 50 percent of the mineral exploration that takes place in B.C. happens on Tahltan land. Mining stretches back to 1861, when gold was discovered in the Stikine River. Swarms of prospectors followed. Mines were built. But until recently, the Indigenous residents were largely ignored, despite a 1910 declaration by the Nation stipulating that those who wished to do business in Tahltan territory would be required to work with the Nation and show respect for its citizens, territory, and rights.

By the late 1980s, mining activity was booming as a result of the Eskay Creek discovery, which had touched off another gold rush. Money raised on the now-defunct Vancouver Stock Exchange was pouring into the region. By contrast, the Tahltan Nation was suffering. About 80 percent of its members were unemployed and many were lost in drug and alcohol addiction. Suicide rates were high and education standards low.

Enter former Chief Jerry Asp, the same man who smuggled Kentucky Fried Chicken into Webequie when he was helping First Nations negotiate in the Ring of Fire. Recognizing that jobs and training would boost prosperity for his people, Asp founded the Tahltan Nation Development

Corporation (TNDC) in 1985. It's now one of the most successful Indigenous-owned businesses in Canada. TNDC has contributed to mine construction, catering, and road building for the Golden Bear, Eskay Creek, and Galore Creek projects and the Red Chris mine. And to the construction of the northwest transmission line featured in Wild's film. For his efforts, Asp was awarded the Queen Elizabeth II Diamond Jubilee Medal in 2013. Four years later, he received the Indspire Award in Business and Commerce, the highest honour the Indigenous community bestows on its own achievers. He was inducted into the Canadian Mining Hall of Fame in 2020.

Now any Tahltan member who wants a job has one. Most jobs are well paid and highly skilled. Training programs abound for those who want to change or advance in their careers.

※

It's 2014. Several Tahltan elders, mostly women, are gathered on the dirt road leading to the Red Chris mine construction project, which is set against the breathtaking backdrop of snow-peaked mountains in north-western B.C. Wild is filming the scene for her documentary. The elders are opposed to the copper-gold mine, distrust its owner, and have set up a blockade to prevent further work. The president of mine owner Imperial Metals and the B.C. minster of Energy and Mines have arrived to discuss solutions. But the elders don't feel ready for the meeting and are refusing to give them an audience.[9]

They are wary because of a recent catastrophic failure of the tailings dam at Imperial's other major asset, the Mount Polley mine near Quesnel Lake. The dam failure released millions of litres of industrial water and slurry containing heavy metals into the lake and other waterways teeming with salmon. It was one of Canada's worst mine disasters.

Trying to mediate between the two parties is the strapping Chad Norman Day, newly elected president of the Tahltan Central Government, the administrative body representing members of the Tahltan Nation living on- and off-reserve. He's a millennial like Noront's Brandyn Chum, just twenty-seven at this moment. At first the elders scold him, as a parent might a child: "Chad, I have to say this to you," offers one of the elders.

"You have never contacted us in a proper manner, you disrespect this blockade and the people. You have a lot to learn and you have to learn to listen to the elders."

Day is firm in his reply: "I believe that our people probably want to hear what the president of Imperial Metals and the minister of Energy and Mines have to say. If we're going to hear them, we need to hear them now."

The conversation proceeds.

Six years later, in 2020, Day speaks to a packed lecture hall at the PDAC convention in Toronto. The TNDC has closed C$3 billion in deals with industry over the past decade, and the Tahltan have become an even more powerful entity. The new majority owner of the Red Chris mine, Australia's Newcrest Mining, is spending C$43 million on contracts with Tahltan businesses in the 2020 fiscal year alone. About half of Newcrest's apprentices at Red Chris hail from the Nation.

But it's a delicate time for Indigenous reconciliation. Not far from Red Chris, Wet'suwet'en hereditary chiefs — leaders whose power is passed down through bloodlines — are opposing the Coastal GasLink pipeline that would carry natural gas to B.C.'s northern coast from the gas fields of northeastern B.C. They have set up blockades to prevent further construction, even though band councils elected under the Indian Act have approved the pipeline. In some interpretations of case law, hereditary chiefs have jurisdiction over territory outside of band-controlled reserves.[10]

Day's four children share Wet'suwet'en heritage, and he is torn. But he argues it's up to each Indigenous community to decide who speaks for them — the elected chief and council or the hereditary chief — and stick to it. "When we want reconciliation with third parties, we need to reconcile ourselves first . . . so we can be united when we go to the outside world and say we don't want this project or we're willing to work with this project. That's not happening right now in a lot of First Nations."

Much to the shock of the band councils, British Columbia eventually sided with the Wet'suwet'en hereditary chiefs, signing a memorandum of understanding that recognizes their authority over the territories. It was a groundbreaking gesture in provincial politics, with the potential to spread nationwide.

The First Nations in the Ring of Fire do not have hereditary chiefs, but they do have some powerful families. They travelled in family units before the Canadian government forced them onto reserves and imposed the band council system with an elected chief for each reserve. Some family names — such as Moonias and Achneepineskum — appear frequently on band leadership rosters, but that does not mean decision-making about developments on Treaty 9 should be left solely to them and other council members, according to Tristan Ashishkeesh, executive director of the Ojibway and Cree Cultural Centre.[11] He says each individual band member should have a say about if and how developments proceed.

The Indigenous population is the youngest and fastest-growing demographic group in Canada, expected to grow from less than 3 percent of the national population in 1996 to about 7 percent in the near future.[12] Even so, the Tahltan's level of clout and prosperity remains out of reach for many Indigenous communities in Canada, including those near the Ring of Fire. The Tahltan, like the Cree of northern Quebec, never ceded their territory to the Crown. So when the time came, they were able to negotiate their own resource deals, their own modern-day treaties. In the James Bay Lowlands, the antiquated and unfair Treaty 9 — though disputed — remains a legal document as of 2022.

✳

Before De Beers closed its Victor mine in May 2019, the company had been excavating some of the most valuable diamonds in the world for eleven years. By then, the host kimberlite pipes — two carrot-shaped plugs of magma that had blasted up from the mantle during the Jurassic age, carrying the spectacular diamonds with them — were clean out of ore. De Beers had identified several more diamond-bearing pipes nearby, but the global powerhouse determined it was not worth its while to mine them, partly because of community resistance to expansion.

That a multinational was digging hundreds of millions of dollars' worth of diamonds from the earth while the community of Attawapiskat, 90 kilometres downriver, suffered from deplorable housing conditions and a youth suicide epidemic had been beyond disturbing. It left a sour taste for many. The relationship might have been better for the Indigenous communities along the west coast of James Bay, and even for De Beers itself, had Canada's environmental assessment process demanded a more rigorous regional approach before any shovels pierced the swampy ground.

According to an article published in the journal *Impact Assessment and Project Appraisal* in 2012, the assessment "took place without any investigations into the most basic land use planning activities." The researchers also found that there was no discussion of broad community development objectives, or if the mine was compatible with them. Regional consultations by both levels of government were lacking.

The relationship between De Beers and Attawapiskat was fraught from the beginning. As early as 2002, the First Nation halted its consultation process with De Beers in the middle of the company's study to determine if the mine was even worth pursuing. The objection was met with surprise by the mining sector, but the First Nation argued that neither the federal nor provincial government had adequately consulted with them as they were legally bound to do.

In late 2005, the two parties finally reached an agreement after both levels of government approved De Beers' environmental assessment for the Victor project. De Beers started building the mine in preparation for commercial production in 2008. Though details of Impact and Benefit Agreements (IBAs) are confidential in Canada, it was later revealed the company agreed to pay Attawapiskat First Nation about C$30 million over the life of the mine.[13] A further C$167 million in contracts was awarded to Indigenous-owned businesses to provide services such as catering and helicopter support, according to the De Beers website.

But the honeymoon didn't last. In 2009, residents of Attawapiskat blockaded the winter road from the mine into the community, arguing that the IBA didn't adequately address a number of pressing issues, including racism and discrimination, pay equity, and the glaring need for new housing and schools. In response, De Beers donated trailers to the community as an emergency measure until more housing could be built. It pledged support in the form of work crews and project management to build a new school in the community to replace squalid learning portables.

On October 28, 2011, Chief Theresa Spence called a state of emergency for the third time in three years over the community's housing situation. Attawapiskat's youth rose up alongside her, launching a social media campaign to draw worldwide attention to the lack of education afforded them. The following year, the federal minister of Aboriginal Affairs announced a contract for a new elementary school that opened in 2014 and cost about C$31 million to build. The government shipped twenty-two modular homes to the community as a more permanent housing solution for families living in tent frames and shacks.

Later that year, Spence upped the ante by launching a six-week hunger strike on an island in the Ottawa River, not far from the Parliament buildings, as part of the Idle No More movement. But her campaign was undermined by an audit of Attawapiskat's books requested by the federal government, and completed by accounting firm Deloitte, that showed the band had not properly accounted for millions of dollars in federal spending from 2005 to 2011.[14]

Meanwhile, trouble was brewing for De Beers and the Victor mine again. A few families who had trap lines running through the vicinity of the area controlled by De Beers sought compensation for the loss of their traditional territory. Others said De Beers should invest directly in community housing, while still others had personal grievances related to past employment or pay. They blocked the winter road carrying supplies to the mine.

At a hearing requested by De Beers in 2013, Timmins Superior Court Judge Robert Riopelle blasted the blockade leaders, labelling them individuals with private financial interests who were holding the corporation to ransom.[15] He said they were not fighting for the community of Attawapiskat, constitutional rights, or land claims, but only for themselves.

The lawyer for De Beers questioned why the Ontario Provincial Police had not arrested the protesters: "What is the message being sent to the world" when "five or six disgruntled ex-employees . . . can shut down a business of 500 people at a cost of millions? That there is no law in northern Ontario?"

In 2015, Spence resigned as chief in order to run for a position on the executive council for the Nishnawbe Aski Nation, representing areas under Treaties 9 and 5 with a total population (on- and off-reserve) of approximately 45,000 people. She lost. She went on a second hunger strike in 2019, the year the Victor mine closed for good, this time to bring attention to her community's lack of potable water and infrastructure as well as its ongoing social struggles.

✳

The Victor mine debacle is a cautionary tale for those hoping to get the much larger Ring of Fire development right. Without widespread support from communities, companies will face blockades at the very least and, at worst, legal challenges that could drag on for years.

Indeed, capital spending on mining projects in Canada is in freefall. By 2021 the projected value of projects planned or under construction for the ten-year period between 2020 and 2030 had dropped to half the C$160 billion projected in 2014. The Mining Association of Canada cites inconsistent and unpredictable domestic policy and regulations of the kind that made the Victor mine so contentious as one of the main reasons for the drop in spending.[16] Canada, once a mining leader, is increasingly seen as a risky jurisdiction to invest dollars earmarked for any form of resource development.

Seeing no end to protests against mining in the James Bay Lowlands, the federal government finally insisted on a regional environmental assessment for the Ring of Fire by the new Impact Assessment Agency of Canada, introduced in 2019. The goal is to capture the cumulative effects of all projects in the region, including social and climate impacts, using a much broader scope than any individual project assessment could achieve. The new framework allows for partnerships with Indigenous communities, considers alternative options and scenarios to determine which projects should go forward, and proposes the best timeline and sequence for mine production. It looks at how adverse impacts could be minimized, not just on a project-by-project basis, but overall.

Even so, Attawapiskat, Fort Albany, and Neskantaga declared a moratorium on development in April 2021, saying the regional environmental assessment was too narrow in focus. Joined by Kashechewan and Eabametoong, they followed up with a letter to federal minister of Environment and Climate Change Steven Guilbeault in January 2022: "What Canada, in agreement with Ontario, plans to do is far from proper or safe, and instead promotes recklessness and danger. Your draft TOR [terms of reference] is narrow in geographic and activity scope, and wrongly excludes us Indigenous peoples from all but token roles."

It may take tweaking, but the new federal process remains an opportunity to transform the Ring of Fire from a contentious boondoggle into a global model for resource development on Indigenous land, a chance for First Nations to drive the resource train. Jean Paul Gladu, an Anishinaabe from Sand Point First Nation, executive director of the Indigenous Resource Network, and a former Noront director, believes it's time to stop arguing and get on with the process despite a lack of full consensus. He wrote in the *Globe and Mail* in late 2021:[17]

> We can't go on like this. Our nations' economic opportunities can't be reduced to a pawn in Canada's political battles.
>
> By paying attention to the extremists on either side we are ignoring the vast majority of Canadians and Indigenous peoples who support responsible resource development, and agree that a fair share of the benefits should go to our nations.
>
> I must also question why our communities need 100 percent support for any project to be deemed credible. We are not a monolith; of course, as in any culture, we too have disagreements. Why are we held to an unreasonable and quite frankly unattainable standard when our current federal system can see a government make decisions on behalf of our entire country with often sub-50 percent support?

Eventually, with better capacity and training opportunities, the First Nations could be empowered to become owners and operators of the mines in the Ring of Fire, not just employed by them. Mining revenues have a way of becoming a form of corporate welfare that mining communities become dependent upon, and an unpredictable one at that. Under a more sustainable model, a healthy portion of the mine profits and decision-making powers would flow to local communities, paving the path to self-governance.

The proposed Ring of Fire development coincides with a growing worldwide demand for minerals for a low-carbon future. Canada is blessed with an abundant supply of nickel, cobalt, lithium, rare earth metals, and other metals and minerals required for the transition to electric, wind, and solar power. In the 2022 budget, the federal government pledged C$3.8 billion towards a critical-minerals strategy, including C$80 million for programs designed to help find the next generation of deposits, C$1.5 billion to invest in new mineral processing and recycling projects, C$103 million for Indigenous engagement and partnerships, and C$1.5 billion towards new infrastructure to reach mineral endowments such as the Ring of Fire. Ontario followed suit in April 2022 with a five-year road map designed to boost the province's critical-minerals supply, including C$12 million from 2023 to 2025 to create a new critical-minerals stream, C$1 billion for related infrastructure, and C$25 million for working capital to Indigenous-owned businesses and entrepreneurs.

Is it such a stretch to imagine a future in which Indigenous businesses in Canada's north supply these critical minerals to a greening world, while living up to their seven-generation promise to protect land and wildlife?

CHAPTER 7

For Peat's Sake

The giraffe couple sauntering towards us was treating us like old friends by now. They'd been visiting almost every day, lazily pulling up alongside the driller, William, and me. Splaying their legs for maximum extension, they liked to bend their long, slender necks down to lap up the residue of pulverized calcrete left over from his labour, presumably because it contained calcium, magnesium, or some other nutrient they craved.

William and I have been investigating the same location at the base of the mountain for weeks, boring through the limey calcrete layer formed by evaporation, then a few metres of solid bedrock. We're working in a grid pattern with the holes spaced tens of metres apart, trying to find extensions of a rich gold system detected a couple of kilometres away on a vast landholding in central Namibia. In particular, we are looking for the contact between dark grey marbles that are mostly barren and lighter grey marbles that host gold invisible to the naked eye.

William is a veteran, manoeuvring the drill as if it were a fifth limb. I'm a freshly hatched geoscientist assigned to document the tiny chips of rocks spitting out of the drill bit. We are both pretty quiet, but we get along okay. Our graceful friends have gifted us an unusual bond. We watch them in awe and admiration.

You'd think the giraffes would be afraid of the noise the percussion drill made as it pounded its way through the soft calcrete into the harder bedrock beneath. The racket was so loud that years later I developed a perennial buzzing in my ears that I couldn't attribute to being the cool kid who attended too many rock concerts.

You'd think they'd be wary of this odd human couple: a sweating, muscled Ovambo man in indigo-blue coveralls manipulating the rig, and his sunburnt colleague of Irish descent in cotton shorts, T-shirt, and wide-brimmed sunhat, squatting on the bleached ground, scribbling in a log book as the rocks revealed themselves one layer at a time.

But these extraordinary herbivores are silently focused on their own goals, swishing their tufty tails to keep the flies away and occasionally batting their luscious eyelashes at us like models in a Maybelline commercial.

❊

In the late 1980s I had the good fortune to land a job as a summer student at Navachab, a gold prospect located in the interior of Namibia, about 200 kilometres northwest of the capital city of Windhoek. Navachab was just beginning to show signs of mineral promise when I touched down on the African continent for the first time in my life, lacking confidence and unsure of where my multinational employer, Anglo American, would send me. I was equally green, having just finished my third of four years studying geoscience at Queen's University in Kingston, Ontario.

Navachab needed personnel, and I needed Navachab. I fell hard for the dusty desert and its natural wonders and even harder for fellow student Roger, a Welshman studying at the University of the Witwatersrand, whose parents had been lured to South Africa in the 1970s from the coal towns of Wales by the promise of prosperity. After I graduated with a BSc in 1986, I jumped at the opportunity to return full-time to Roger and to this dynamic project amid the blood-red mountains of Namibia's central plateau.

Before it became a gold prospect, Navachab had been a private game reserve and remained so throughout the exploration phase of the project. Entries such as this one in the diary *Navachab Chronicles* were commonplace:

> At the reservoir, Dave found large and dinkum [genuine]
> leopard tracks. The old windmill pump on the way to Anomaly

16 has been restored to working order and mountain zebras are regular partakers there now. The various salt licks that have been distributed around the farm are being used, a sizable group of young kudu observed at one . . . [and] not half an hour ago, a young baboon was brave enough to venture just behind the core yard, eating red gum from the tree.[1]

Our team grew accustomed to being pelted with rocks by baboons while mapping the geology of the surrounding mountains. Whenever they sensed us coming, the primates would line up along the mountain ridge, barking at the top of their lungs, their hairy silhouettes forming an intimidating army. Then, as if prompted by a "fire!" signal from the alpha male, they'd launch a barrage of stones until we backed off. Lucky for us, they had lousy aim.

Equally commonplace were the puff adders sunning their fat brown chevroned bodies on the camp road as we passed by on our twilight runs, kicking dust in their faces. Puff adders are responsible for most of the snakebite fatalities in Africa, according to *A Field Guide to the Reptiles of East Africa*. But they're usually indifferent to humans. They prefer to wait in camouflage for smaller prey and, unlike most snakes, couldn't be bothered to slither away at the sound of footfall. So it's easy to step on them by accident and then, of course, all hell breaks loose.

More than once we encountered a spitting cobra in the camp kitchen. These snakes liked to cool off from the desert heat on the room's concrete floor. There's nothing quite as terrifying as going for a cuppa and finding yourself trapped in an enclosed space with a rearing reptile trying to blind you with spit before going in for the kill.

In the temporary satellite tent camps we erected to investigate more remote prospects lurked other dangers. Scorpions liked to curl up in our warm boots in the chill of the desert night. We had to remember to shake out our footwear every morning to avoid a bite that burns like hot coals. And while scorpions sought warmth, shyer leopards might use the cloak of darkness to pad around the camp with curiosity. We'd sometimes spot their tracks at sunrise.

My fellow geoscientists and I knew how lucky we were to live and work in a wildlife paradise, despite these occasional risky encounters.

And so our excitement was mixed with growing unease as the drilling started yielding consistently excellent gold grades. Visits from head office in Johannesburg became more frequent as the company managers realized they had a potential gold mine on their hands. After briefing them on our fieldwork, we'd pile the visiting brass in our white Toyota Land Cruisers and take them on a tour of Navachab's latest exploration hot spots, pointing out herds of galloping zebra and bouncing springbok along the way, partly hoping they'd return home unimpressed by our progress.

※

The ongoing battle of nature versus development in the Ring of Fire is an existential crisis felt by mineral explorers the world over. They tend to be wilderness lovers, attracted to fieldwork precisely because of an appreciation for nature and the outdoors, not in spite of it. They know discovery success has the potential to create wealth for surrounding communities but also to inflict environmental degradation. Weighing the silence, majesty, and wildlife of the bush against the potential impacts of mining is a difficult reckoning.

Unlike the cinematic deserts and stunning wildlife of Namibia, the swampy flats of the James Bay Lowlands do not appear on tourists' bucket lists. Any trees that do grow in the southern reaches are stunted from lack of sunlight and poor soil conditions. In the northern half lie vast stretches of muskeg, mostly impenetrable by human or animal, yet swarming with bloodsucking bugs. The air is damp, the winds off the inland seas of James and Hudson Bay bone-chillingly cold. The sun rarely shines. Colours are muted.

And yet underneath this bleak veneer lies a rich and fragile ecosystem. Fish and other water creatures thrive in the clean, clear rivers that flow from the majestic rock faces of the Canadian Shield to the west. During fall migration, the James Bay coastline supports up to 20 percent of the populations of several shorebird species, including an endangered long-distance flyer called the red knot. This is the only area between the maritime Arctic and the Gulf of St. Lawrence and the Atlantic and the Gulf of Mexico that offers a tidal saltwater habitat for them.[2] Eelgrass, sedges, and marsh grasses provide important food sources for the waterfowl. Even larger mammals such as bear, caribou, lynx, and moose find enough to eat to stick around. Venture much further north, beyond the Attawapiskat River watershed where the Victor diamond mine once operated and the Ring of Fire deposits lie, and you're in polar bear country.

Even less obvious are the remarkable qualities of the region's peat-lands.

The value of peat — a brown, spongy material resembling soil — as a carbon store was a key talking point at the twenty-sixth UN Climate Change Conference in November 2021. "The climate crisis will not be resolved without attention to the essential role of nature . . . proactive safeguarding of peatland carbon stores can have enormous co-benefits by conserving biodiversity and ecosystem integrity, potentially at vast scales," Dr. Lorna Harris, post-doctoral researcher at the University of Alberta, said in an address to politicians and scientists.

And guess where you find a quarter of the world's peatlands? In Canada, most abundantly in the Hudson Bay and James Bay Lowlands. The 320,000–square-kilometre area is the second-largest temperate wetland in the world.[3] It is also one of the last undammed watersheds in North America, its rivers a source of critical nutrients and organic material. The Ring of Fire, otherwise known as the McFaulds Lake greenstone belt, underlies about 5,000 square kilometres or 1.6 percent of this vast region.

As described in Chapter 1, when the Laurentide Ice Sheet retreated thousands of years ago, the Tyrrell Sea flooded the basin around Hudson Bay, depositing layers of sediments on top of debris from previous glaciers. As the heavy ice continued to melt, the land bounced back in a phenomenon called isostatic rebound. The sea receded, leaving behind a flat, impermeable surface.

Tidal marshes flourished under these conditions. And as the land continued to spring back, swamp forests and then bogs ("a wet spongy ground unable to support any heavy body"[4]) emerged. Plants and lichens sucked carbon dioxide from the atmosphere to store in their roots and leaves. When the vegetation died and decomposed, carbon was seques-tered in peat. To this day, as microbes in the peat soil digest plant matter, they release carbon dioxide and methane back into the atmosphere. But the waterlogged, oxygen-deprived, permafrosted nature of the peat ensures a barely perceptible, slow-motion release.[5]

This type of peatland has other unique properties. Like a giant sponge, it can hold up to thirty times its own weight in water. Ecologist John Riley, a leading expert on the lowlands, once calculated there was as much water there as in the Great Lakes, just spread out over the land. The peat filters contaminants from the water and prevents wildfires too.

The Attawapiskat River watershed encompassing the Ring of Fire area, one of several district watersheds in the lowlands, is characterized by bog and fen ("a tract of low land covered wholly or partially with water"[6]). A myriad of open pools surrounds this wet spongy ground. In relatively well-drained areas, sphagnum mosses cover about half the surface and lichen the other half. Hummocks scattered amid the bog anchor stunted black spruce mixed with tamarack. The peat has accumulated to a depth of as much as three metres here.

As far as European settlers were concerned, swamps like this were inhospitable landscapes that harboured pathogens and possibly even ghosts and ghouls. If they stood in the way of development, they had to go. In 1793, U.S. president George Washington and his cronies went so far as to form the Great Dismal Swamp Company to drain a vast peatland on the Virginia–North Carolina border that William Byrd II (the founder of Richmond, Virginia) described as "a miserable morass where nothing can inhabit." The company believed "draining, improving and saving the land" would make way for arable real estate,[7] dismissing the fact that Indigenous people had been thriving in the swamp for thousands of years. When that plan failed, the Great Dismal Swamp Company forced enslaved labourers to build a canal through the swamp to facilitate trade. It wasn't until nearly 200 years later that the Dismal Swamp Act of 1974 directed the U.S. Fish and Wildlife Service to protect and preserve what little was left of this unique ecosystem and the diversity of animal and plant life within.

Central Park in New York City was once bog and fen, too, and public health authorities worried that the malodorous miasma emanating from rotting organic matter was causing cholera outbreaks in the city in the mid-nineteenth century. The bog was drained in the 1850s to create parkland. Many other cities followed suit, draining and paving over their wetlands to rid themselves of the stench produced by anerobic bacteria, and to create conduits for the flow of sewage and other waste.

Peatlands got a bad rap, one they're only just beginning to shake.

✳

The hidden beauty of these waterlogged ecosystems is that they don't change much under normal conditions. That stability makes them valuable sinks or storehouses of carbon, mercury, and other potentially troublesome materials. Peatlands cover only 3 percent of the earth's surface but store more carbon than other types of ecosystems. A square metre of peatland in the Hudson Bay Lowland, for instance, contains about five times the amount of carbon as one square metre of tropical rainforest in the Amazon, according to the Wildlife Conservation Society. On top of that, peat sequesters more than 12 megatons of carbon dioxide each year; Ontario's annual carbon dioxide emissions are around 170 megatons.[8]

But what if this slow and steady ecosystem were to be disrupted by human activity or a warming climate? Like an evil genie escaping its bottle, the ecosystem could easily tip into a different feedback system that releases these sequestered substances into the water and atmosphere.

Climate change is expected to hit particularly hard in the James Bay Lowlands. A shorter ice cover season on Hudson Bay and James Bay is leading to longer, warmer summers and shorter winters. Permafrost is melting. Wildfires are increasing. The hydrology of the area is about to change irrevocably as more water floods the system, while at the same time evapotranspiration leaves behind drier soils. Eventually, tonnes of carbon stored in the peatlands will be released as the permafrost vanishes and the microbes ramp up their activity under more encouraging conditions. Wildlife will struggle to survive.

Climate change, ironically, exacerbates the need for more all-weather road building to the north as the season for winter roads to communities shrinks. But road building also threatens to disrupt the peat soils and create year-round truck traffic. It's imperative to evaluate the potential to damage the carbon sequestering and biodiversity contributions of this globally significant peatland before construction begins.

Beyond the disturbance of the peatlands and its wildlife habitats, there are other environmental hazards of mining, including dust, noise, and water and air pollution. The worst of all is a tailings dam failure. Tailings are waste material left over after the rock has been crushed and the valuable minerals extracted. The dam is an earthen structure built to store the tailings. Depending on the type of mine, tailings can contain toxic elements such as heavy metals or sulphides. There have been several dam failures worldwide, but two immediately come to mind: Mount Polley in British Columbia and Córrego do Feijão in Brazil.

In the early morning hours of August 4, 2014, the dam at the Mount Polley copper-gold mine collapsed, releasing 17 million tonnes of water and 5 million tonnes of waste material into Quesnel Lake, Hazeltine Creek, and other area waterways in northwestern B.C.[9] An independent panel investigating the disaster concluded that the breach was the result of both a design flaw that centred the pond over unstable glacial debris and a mistake in construction.[10] The failure could have been averted if the operator, Imperial Metals, had followed the original design, including a gentler slope on the downstream side of the dam. Two engineers involved in the embankment design and monitoring were disciplined for unprofessional conduct. Years later, Quesnel Lake was still showing elevated levels of copper and fine sediment with the potential to affect fish growth, reproduction, and survival and alter algae communities, despite the C$70 million spent on remediation by Imperial Metals.

In Brazil, the consequences of carelessness were much deadlier. In early January 2019, 270 people were killed when a tailings dam failed at the Córrego do Feijão iron ore mine, releasing a mudflow that covered the mine's offices and several private residences downstream. About half of the victims were employees of mine owner Vale, the same company that owns and operates many of the nickel mines in Sudbury (after purchasing Inco in 2006). The Brazilian National Water Agency said the tailings could pollute over 300 kilometres of river. A regional labour judge ordered Vale to pay US$197,240 in compensation to each family of the 131 employees killed. In total the company agreed to pay almost US$40 billion in claims, though it is unclear how much of that has actually been distributed.

Such a spill would damage the fragile ecosystem that hosts the Ring of Fire. Even an arguably lesser evil, the acid mine drainage that forms when sulphide-rich rocks are broken down by exposure to water and air at the surface, can damage local streams and groundwater for miles around if they are not treated with care. These potential dangers are why Noront, after consulting with the First Nations in the region, proposed that all tailings from the Eagle's Nest operation be placed back into the underground voids left by mining. This solution would prevent contamination of surface water courses and eliminate the chances of a tailings dam failure. Risk to groundwater would be mitigated by mixing the tailings with a cemented paste so that water would flow around, rather than through, the tailings.

The company also proposed using only underground development in the region, to prevent the ugly and often lingering impact of open cast mining on the landscape. Open cast mines can take up vast amounts of space, and the dust and noise emanating from them make the surrounding region inhospitable to wildlife. Even with rehabilitation, it can take decades for an open pit to recover enough vegetation to revert to a less altered state. Underground mines, by contrast, are largely hidden beneath the surface and can be transformed close to their original condition once the ore has been exploited.

But Noront is no longer in charge. Responsibility for the environment passed on to Noront's acquirer Wyloo Metals in 2022. Fortescue, Wyloo's owner in Australia, made a net income of more than A$7 billion in 2020 mining iron ore and belched out about 2 million tonnes of greenhouse gases in the process.[11] Founder and chairman Andrew "Twiggy" Forrest plans to revolutionize his company by aiming for carbon neutrality by 2030 and producing five times as much renewable energy, including green hydrogen, than the Australian power grid.

"The [fossil fuel] party's over. I know it. You know it," a confident, smiling Twiggy said in a video to promote his hydrogen energy dreams.

Hopefully, for the sake of all stakeholders, Forrest's recent efforts to clean up his act will amount to more than just greenwashing.

✳

Against all odds — gold discoveries rich enough to become mines are extremely rare — our Navachab evolved into an open-pit operation in 1989, producing 65,000 to 80,000 ounces of gold (worth about US$125 million) annually. That same year, Roger and I relocated to Toronto to continue our careers in Canada, partly so that Roger could dodge mandatory service fighting border wars in South Africa's apartheid-era army. Navachab is expected to continue churning out gold until at least 2028.

Amost two decades after our relocation, we returned to the site where we'd first met as geoscientists in training. The labyrinth of paved roads, massive open pits, processing plants, and tight security was hardly recognizable to us. The development, devoid of both the beauty and wildlife we remembered, summoned feelings of sadness tinged with a complicated pride in the enterprise.

I was relieved to hear that the giraffes who'd kept us company on the drill rig so many years ago had survived and procreated. The new mine owners were protecting their descendants at a nearby plot, or so they told us. Although giraffes are not an endangered species in Namibia, the animal received vulnerable status in 2016 on the International Union for the Conservation of Nature's Red List of Threatened Species.

The tailings dumps from the gold mining process were being rehabilitated, with a study showing that some of the former dumps support a diversity of plants, insects, and larger mammals.[12]

And the Navachab mine has brought a generation of economic prosperity to surrounding communities by employing hundreds of people and providing taxes to support infrastructure in the country. As the mine moved underground for the first time in 2021, many in the region hoped it would provide several more years of economic contributions.

It can be a maddening exercise to weigh economic benefits against environmental concerns. Trying to find a balance is next to impossible. Exploration geoscientists have the unique privilege of being able to work in the wilderness, cover up their tracks, and move on to the next prospect without causing much damage. Stakeholders who inherit their successes do not.

CHAPTER 8

Sudbury 2.0

James Hodgins steps gingerly around his tripod and heads for a spotlight he's arranged to illuminate the gloom. He adjusts the beam's angle then sloshes over to fiddle with the modifiers meant to soften and spread the light and bring out the best in his subjects. The instruments' delicate legs are lodged in muck just viscous enough to keep them from toppling over. James pauses in a tight stance, palms stretched forward as an imaginary safeguard.

Okay, all set.

Returning to his camera, he mops sweat from his prescription safety glasses with his neckerchief before peering through the viewfinder. His hardhat is loaded with a miner's light and feels heavy in the humid air, as if it were slowly crushing the upper vertebrae of his spine.

Looming in front of James is his subject: a yellow scoop tram the size of a house. The beast has the capacity to lift up to 18 tonnes of dynamite blasted ore — more than the weight of two bull elephants — in its cavernous maw, then carry the rumbling payload through the underground labyrinth of the mine and dump it down the dark tunnel of the ore pass to the depths below.

This tram is special: it's outfitted with a laser that works in conjunction with a built-in camera to determine the vehicle's location, how fast it is moving, and how widely it needs to turn. Using Bluetooth technology, a human can operate the tram from the surface, eliminating the need for a driver and, with that, the safety hazards and monotony associated with operating large machinery underground. It's one of the first of its kind in the world, inanimate but deemed worthy of a portrait sitting by its owners.

An army of miners, managers, and communicators in matching tangerine coveralls glowing with reflector tape is gathered around James, ventilators dangling from their hip belts, watching him set up, waiting for their turn in front of the lens. He feels their impatience, their eyes boring though his hardhat. Every inactive minute in a mine means lost profit and a thinner bonus for the miners. Everyone is keen to get back to work.

Now is not the time to rush, James reminds himself. Pretend they're not there. Pretend those shadows are just moist patches on the mine floor. Come on, James, focus.

Because if James doesn't get the shot now, he won't have another chance. He is stationed more than a kilometre underground. It has taken considerable time and expense to transport him there from his home in Sudbury, Ontario. He can't screw it up.

✳

About 1.8 billion years ago, Earth was a moody young adult. Oxygen was building in the atmosphere as the planet recovered from the latest deep-freeze. Microscopic single-celled organisms were beginning to multiply in the otherwise empty oceans. But the land remained a red, rocky, inhospitable place, sunburnt and sullen.

Then, suddenly and violently, a giant dusty snowball of a comet from outer space disturbed that silence, slamming into the earth's crust at thousands of kilometres per hour close to what is now known as Sudbury.

The impact punched a hole in the crust and released enough heat to melt all the rock in the vicinity, leaving a boiling cauldron of magma about five kilometres deep. The resulting shock waves shattered the rocks for miles around. Geologists reckon the molten rock in the crater reached a temperature of 1727 degrees Celsius and bubbled away at temperatures above 1000 degrees for up to a quarter of a million years.[1]

While the soup was simmering, the heavy metal–rich liquids within were sinking to the uneven crater floor, settling into depressions and seeping into cracks in the surrounding rock. As the heavy liquid cooled, it rained out the nickel, copper, and platinum group metal deposits that would be mined hundreds of millions of years later.

Eventually, like a cake removed from the oven before its time, the crater collapsed in on itself, forming a 200-kilometre diameter hole in the ground. Squeezed by the powerful forces of the ever-shifting earth and eroded by wind and weather, the crater later shrunk to a tidy 60-by-30-kilometre ellipse that can be seen from space today.

This ellipse is known as the Sudbury Basin or the Sudbury Structure. It is still the third-largest known impact crater on Earth, and one of the oldest. The metal endowment within is renowned worldwide for its richness.

✳

James stuffs his overnight bag under the seat in front of him and flops down next to me in the beaten-up old twin prop. There's a deafening roar as we barrel down the runway. Then we're airborne, the plane's wings seesawing wildly in the wind, a checkerboard of fields spreading out below us as we head towards northern Canada. Even though we've experienced this kind of liftoff countless times before, there's no getting used to the sensation of being tossed around by air currents in a winged vehicle not much bigger than a mine truck. It's like the carnival ride you didn't anticipate would be quite so nauseating when you eagerly joined the queue.

With his logo emblazoned across his jacket, camera bag, and, who knows, maybe even his socks and underwear, James is a walking brand. But he has an enthusiasm for his work I rarely encounter on these junkets. My travelling cohort usually consists of research analysts invited from banks and brokerage houses in Toronto and Vancouver to evaluate mines and mineral exploration projects around the world on behalf of investors. They do interesting work and make oodles of money, but often grow weary of their battle with time zones and the toll it takes on their health and family life. But James, a decade my junior, is like a kid on his first adventure.

When we finally arrive at our motel with the appetites of soldiers just back from an all-day march, there's a boil-water advisory in effect. No matter, I try to convince myself, there's enough beer at the bar to quench any traveller's thirst. At least we have a solid roof over our heads, never a given on these trips to the beyond. We shower, trying hard not to swallow, change into our evening wear of jeans and T-shirts, and collapse into bar chairs to discuss our mission ahead as the creative team.

Early the next morning, we make our way to the mine site and take in the mandatory safety briefing for visitors. We get kitted out in coveralls, hardhats, and Elmer Fudd boots designed to wade through the muck. James has supplied his own kit, but he won't get off that easily. In order to guarantee a tight fit for the ventilator that will keep his lungs free of dust, he's had to shave off a big part of his identity, his beard.

Despite feeling a lesser version of himself, baby-faced James is cheerful when he hops in the Toyota Land Cruiser, retrofitted paddy wagon–style for safety. Once everyone is perched side by side on the cold, hard benches, the driver starts the descent down the gently winding ramp to the bowels of the mine. Hard-hatted heads knock against each other as we move silently through the darkness like a pity of prisoners being transported back to their dungeon. Even though the mine is less than two kilometres deep, we travel a distance of about fourteen kilometres when all the twists and turns along the underground switchback are taken into account. The Eagle's Nest mine plan in the Ring of Fire follows a similar design: a portal at surface leading to a spiralling ramp down to the lowest production levels.

After all that, James gets his scoop tram shot, hops in the mine cage to surface with the afternoon shift change, climbs out of his mine outfit and into his civvies, and begins the long journey home to Sudbury.

✳

The rich deposits of metal that formed around Sudbury as a result of the earth-shattering violence of the space rock's impact slumbered for hundreds of millions of years as the world evolved around them. Continents joined together and split apart again. Single-celled organisms became multicellular life, then evolved into jellyfish-like animals. Around half a billion years ago, a few creatures started swimming around under their own steam and the first true vertebrates, looking a lot like slippery eels, appeared. But they stuck to the safety of the oceans, unconcerned with the odd volcanic eruption taking place on the desolate land around them.

Another 100 million years or so passed by. The first four-legged creatures appeared and proliferated on land as birds, mammals, and reptiles. A mass extinction around 250 million years ago put an end to that party but gave rise to the dinosaur era. The dinosaurs, in turn, were eventually exterminated by the clouds of noxious dust and smoke that enveloped Earth after another giant space rock crash-landed 65 million years ago.

Still, the Sudbury ores slept.

Tens of millions of years later, for better or worse, humans emerged and started walking on two legs,[2] unaware their descendants would become dependent on the metals beneath their feet for their livelihood.

They didn't find their way to the Sudbury area until about 11,000 years ago as the last of the glaciers retreated. Called Plano (of the plains), the new arrivals were big game hunters and among the first humans adept at chipping stone. They began quarrying quartzite on Manitoulin Island in the Georgian Bay just southwest of Sudbury, crafting the stone into tools and weapon heads. The Plano evolved into the Shield (of the Canadian Shield) Culture that became dominant in northern Ontario.

The Shields discovered copper in the area and used it to fashion not only tools and weapons, but jewellery and ornaments they could trade. Based on what's known about the locations of their settlements along waterways, they must have been mobile, probably travelling by birchbark canoe. They established trading routes with other bands, most notably their Shield sisters to the south. They are considered the likely ancestors of the Ojibway, Cree, Algonquin, and Montagnais.[3]

The Ojibway went on to become the dominant culture in the region. They typically moved among temporary encampments to fish and hunt. When the French established a major fur-trading centre in Sault Ste. Marie (where the Great Lakes Superior and Huron meet) in the mid-seventeenth century, the Ojibway became increasingly interested in what the Europeans had to offer. Eager to trade, various bands competed for the best hunting grounds, leading to competition and conflict among them.[4]

But the real troublemakers for the Ojibway were not the French, who mostly just wanted their furs, but the English, who kept settling down and making inquiries about the metals in the area. As settlers began arriving in larger and larger numbers in the early nineteenth century, the Ojibway grew increasingly concerned. They complained to the British colonial government about trespassing. Their complaints were ignored.

Perhaps if Ojibway Chief Shawenakeshick had known what the area would soon become and how mining would affect the lives of his people, he wouldn't have signed the Robinson-Huron Treaty that sealed his Nation's fate in 1850. The treaty was similar to Treaty 9, signed by the Indigenous peoples of the James Bay Lowlands to the north decades later. In exchange for a one-time lump sum and annual payments that were supposed to increase from time to time based on profits generated from mining and forestry in the area, the Ojibway agreed to share their lands and resources with the newcomers.

In what's become a familiar treaty story, there has been lots of profitable mining and forestry, but not an increase in the annuity since 1874.

"As settlers and their representatives increased their control over lands and resources in the colony, it became clear that they were quite prepared to disregard aboriginal rights," according to a case study of the Robinson treaties prepared for the Royal Commission on Aboriginal Peoples.[5]

In 2014, twenty-one Robinson-Huron chiefs launched a lawsuit that exposed this injustice. The case took six years to wind its way through the courts, but Justice Patricia Hennessy eventually ruled in mid-2020 that Canada and Ontario had failed to live up to their obligations to increase the annuity payments.[6] The judge blamed the reluctance of both governments to take responsibility for the compensation: provinces control resource decisions, while responsibility for First Nations rests with the federal government.

"This century-old dispute between the federal and provincial Crowns is one of the reasons why no increase has been made to the annuities for over 150 years," said Hennessy in the decision. "This delay has had enormous negative consequences for the plaintiffs, not the least of which is the cost and complications of litigating this dispute based on two centuries of evidence. It is the stage on which this dispute plays out."

✳

A few years after the Robinson-Huron Treaty was written into law, a surveyor, W.A. Salter, was running a line north near Whitefish Lake, now an Ojibway community on the edge of Sudbury, when his compass suggested a "considerable local attraction, the needle varying between four to fourteen degrees westerly."[7] A fellow surveyor, Alexander Murray, had a similar experience.

Between them, they determined that a large iron ore body must be messing with their compass needles. But when they sampled the surrounding outcrop, they discovered pyrite (iron sulphide), a mineral often associated with nickel and copper mineralization. Salter and Murray reported the information to the Geological Survey of Canada,[8] but their findings were never investigated.

The Sudbury treasure remained, once again, a deeply buried secret revealing only the subtlest hints of its bounty.

Finally, in 1883, a crew was blasting its way through the bedrock of northern Ontario to build the transcontinental railway that would connect the new country of Canada. Legend has it that, during the blasting, a blacksmith noticed a rust-coloured patch of rock, a telltale sign of sulphide mineralization and, often, metals.

Sure enough, samples from the rock cut returned high concentrations of copper at the assay lab. Settlers moved quickly to tie up all the prospective ground. By 1886, the Canadian Copper Company was producing copper and nickel and shipping it to a smelter in New Jersey for refinement. A new mining centre was born.

The city that was to become Sudbury (named after the hometown of the rail construction superintendent's wife in Suffolk, England) was never meant to be more than a temporary camp for the Canadian Pacific Railway workers. But the area quickly became famous for having some of the world's largest deposits of nickel, copper, and platinum group metals. More settlers flocked there, drawn by the seemingly endless riches the abominable fireball from space had created.

By the end of the twentieth century, prospectors had found some 116 different metal deposits in the Sudbury Basin[9] and the population had swelled to 150,000. About half of the Allies' artillery manufactured for World War II used nickel from the Sudbury mines. The deposits have produced an estimated C$500 billion worth of metal. Several deposits continue to yield ore. Sudbury also plays an important role in the Ring of Fire story: Richard Nemis was born and raised in the northern town; Noront had its beginnings there; and the concentrates flowing from Eagle's Nest and other potential nickel mines in the area will likely one day end up in the region's smelters.

✳

The Ojibway who had thrived in the region before the 1883 railway-cut discovery either dispersed into southern Ontario and beyond (perhaps choked out by pollution), were decimated by infectious disease, or became dependent on the settlers for their livelihoods. With the Indian Act of 1876 the government took control over their status, land, resources, and education. The failure of the Crown to keep up their side of the bargain regarding annuities from mining and forestry pushed the Ojibway further into poverty. On the contrary, many settlers thrived. One was Richard Nemis's father. He helped build the town's first smokestacks before founding Noront Steel.

The smokestacks rose above Sudbury's nickel smelters like lonely sentinels, belching pollution into the pristine northern air. By 1960, Sudbury had become the largest point source of sulphur dioxide in the world, with annual emissions peaking at approximately 2.5 million tonnes.[10] The air pollution was so wretched that residents of nearby Happy Valley, where many of the Falconbridge workers resided, were forced by the government to evacuate. They left behind a ghost town that never quite lived up to its name.

The environmental impacts were devastating. The forests died, leaving a barren landscape almost the size of Hong Kong, looking not dissimilar to the desolate scene of 1.8 billion years previous. About 7,000 local lakes became acidic when the sulphur fell as acid rain, killing fish and eventually rendering the water bodies inhospitable to life. It was a dystopian filmmaker's dreamscape.

There were social costs too, beyond the decimation of Ojibway life and culture. The contentious relationship among the two main operators, "Mother Inco" and "Falco," and the union representing the miners led to decades of labour strife. Vulnerable to the vagaries of the metals market, the operators would sometimes shutter operations when metal prices were low, throwing thousands out of work with no pay.

By 1962, there were 17,000 men working in Falconbridge's nickel mine and Inco's seven mines and two smelters,[11] all members of the Mine Mill Union. Mine Mill was condemned by the Canadian Labour Congress as a communist organization and was eventually forced to merge with the United Steelworkers union that was making incursions into Sudbury. But not before a battle between the two factions ripped the community apart.

In 1966, labour dissatisfaction exploded into violence, including knifings, vandalism, and bombings. About 200 Ontario Provincial Police officers were called in to quell the striking crowd. It was around this time that the late singer and songwriter Stompin' Tom Connors wrote his famous "Sudbury Saturday Night." Resentment towards Inco, a company that both patronized its miners and controlled their livelihoods while pocketing about C$150 million in profits per year, was palpable. Drinking at the bar until their eyes began to twinkle offered a temporary reprieve from a Kafkaesque world.

But the strike empowered the steelworkers to negotiate a new pay package, making the Sudbury miners among the highest paid in the world. Another four-month strike in 1969 yielded even greater benefits, including a prescription drug plan, an insurance plan, and a cost-of-living allowance as well as better pensions, all commonplace now for miners in Canada.[12]

The companies and the union settled into an uneasy relationship, but it wasn't long before the strife re-emerged like a cancer coming out of remission. In 1972, Inco laid off hundreds of miners, a move the union considered an attempt to weaken them just before wage and benefit negotiations were set to get underway.

"Every time our guys start negotiating a new contract with 'Mother Inco,' they call for a layoff," one miner told the *New York Times*. "We thought things had changed since the 1969 strike. Now we know better."[13]

In August 1982, Prime Minister Pierre Trudeau was on vacation, travelling across Canada with his three sons, Alexandre, Michel, and future PM Justin, then just ten years old. The prime minister had recently finished repatriating Canada's constitution and was using the Governor General's deluxe train car for a self-congratulatory trip to the Rockies. Canada was in the midst of a recession, unemployment had reached historic highs, and people were losing their homes as a result of interest rates as high as 19 percent.

At Salmon Arm, B.C., the prime minister's entourage was met with placard-waving protesters pointing out the hypocrisy of his luxury train trip while the rest of the country suffered. To shield the first family from the angry mob, a staff member began lowering the window blinds, according to the *Salmon Arm Observer*. But, while his children giggled, the prime minister raised the blinds and glared out at the protesters.

"He looked at my wife, he smiled and gave her the finger. He pushed up the other blind, looked at me and gave me the finger," protester Doug Hughes later told the Canadian Press.[14]

As the train lumbered eastward, more angry Canadians emerged. They pelted the rail car with tomatoes and other debris.

But nothing prepared Trudeau for the scene that awaited him in Sudbury. Nor far along the track from where the CPR blasting crew had discovered the Sudbury ore deposits in 1883, a crowd of about five hundred residents facing 20 percent unemployment levels threw rocks, eggs, and tomatoes at the coach, breaking two windows. The day before the demonstration, Inco had announced 1,050 more layoffs, reducing the workforce to 8,900, almost half what it was a decade previous.

This game of chicken between Inco and the union lasted right up until 2006, when Vale, a Brazilian iron ore producer, purchased Inco for C$19.4 billion. Three years after the takeover, the miners joined the picket line again. If the union members thought Inco was one tough mother, they hadn't seen anything yet.

"It's a war zone here," millwright and picket captain James Joudrey, who was leading the strike against Vale, told the *Toronto Star*'s Tony Van Alphen in 2009. "[Vale's] tactics are designed to provoke us like never before. They're not interested in getting back to bargaining."

Unsurprisingly, the talks failed, resulting in a year-long strike, the longest in the union's history. Vale kept production going during the strike using non-union and replacement workers, something Inco — despite its other transgressions — had never done. There was even a rumour that Vale was flying Brazilians into the mine sites by helicopter to replace the striking Canadians.

The United Steelworkers Local 6500 would never regain its strength after that humiliating defeat. The union's numbers now fluctuate in the 2,500–3,000 range, representing a majority of production and maintenance workers in mining, milling, smelting, and refining at Vale's operations in Sudbury.

The upside of all this despair is that Sudbury residents are no longer reliant on the one or two mining companies for employment. In the 1970s, 25 percent or more of the local workforce worked for Inco.[15] Now, less than 5 percent work directly in mining, and Sudbury is considered a bona fide metropolis, the cultural and business hub of Ontario's North. The city has become self-sustaining, with thriving education, tourism, health care, and a globally renowned mining supply and service sector. Even the landscape around Sudbury has healed from the horrific wounds inflicted by the smelter smokestacks, though not without scar tissue.

In 1985, Ontario ordered the Sudbury smelters, among other operations, to curtail sulphur production. The bold move impressed even Americans accustomed to viewing Canada as an irrelevant backwater. U.S. Senator George J. Mitchell of Maine said Ontario "has now done more in a single day to reduce acid rain than the Reagan Administration has done in five years."[16]

Seven years later, Sudbury won an award at the UN Earth Summit for its community-led revitalization effort to plant ten million trees. Fish in the lakes within and beyond the city limits began to thrive again. In 2015, Statistics Canada named Sudbury the happiest city in Canada after more than 45 percent of the city's residents rated their quality of life a 9 out of 10. Happy Valley was back.

In 2016 the Sudbury Neutrino Observatory (SNOLAB), housed in Vale's Creighton mine more than two kilometres below ground, jointly won the US$3 million Breakthrough Prize in Fundamental Physics. The international prize recognized SNOLAB for its contribution to the understanding of neutrinos, fleeting particles produced in nuclear reactions that are almost impossible to detect. The lab's leader, physicist Art McDonald, won a Nobel Prize for his groundbreaking scientific work.

When most people think of mining communities, they think of exploitative companies exacerbating the natural boom-bust resource cycle by greedily lining their pockets during good times and doing nothing to keep people housed and employed during downturns. After decades of hard-fought union battles, a wholesale clean-up of the environment, and a more diversified workforce independent of the mines, Sudbury is an example of a mining community that has overcome this damaging whiplash.

It's not perfect — stricter pollution regulations in the province threw Sudbury's two smelters back into non-compliance in 2020 — but Sudbury is a mining town that has evolved into something much greater than its origins.

James the photographer is a poster boy for Sudbury's economic diversification. He makes a living at photography, a career few can afford to pursue even in the world's major centres, because with the advent of high-quality phone cameras everyone and their grandmother has become a photographer. He's captured a lot of milestones for Sudbury residents: their births, their weddings, their deaths.

As a child, James remembers scrambling up and down Sudbury's smooth black rock, the famous "moonscape" created by emissions from the smaller smokestacks that dominated the skyline, belching out clouds of acid and metal and killing off life for miles around. The area was so barren that NASA chose Sudbury as an astronaut training ground for the Apollo moon missions. Now he spends his summer weekends in the lush wilderness surrounding the city, fishing in the clean waters of the region's many lakes.

His grandfathers both worked indirectly for the mining sector, one as a security guard at Lockerby nickel mine, the other for CP Rail. His father also worked for a mining company, and as a kid, James assumed he would continue the legacy. But after taking a photography course at college he was smitten. He learned the art of photography at an agency, then spun off on his own to brand himself as a mining photographer. A decade later, he travels the world photographing miners and their equipment for magazines, marketing materials, and internal company communications. In a way he's gone full circle: making use of his deep mining roots to sustain his creative passion.

✳

Comparisons have been drawn between the mineral deposits of Sudbury and those of the Ring of Fire. They both contain metals valued in the hundreds of millions. They harbour similar commodities: mostly nickel, copper, platinum group metals, and gold, with the bonus of chromium in the Ring of Fire. They lie within 1,000 kilometres of each other in the vast province of Ontario and on traditional Ojibway territory.

But what are the chances of a creative class of writers, musicians, and photographers like James sprouting around the Ring of Fire? Could a Ring of Fire community emulate Sudbury's success while avoiding the city's descent into environmental and social hell?

A lot about the way the mining industry operates has changed in the century or so since Sudbury found its legs. Now, instead of establishing company towns, operators generally prefer a fly-in, fly-out model, where employees work for fourteen days straight followed by a one- or two-week break, or some version of that rotation. The camps are temporary but generally comfortable, many with skilled chefs, domestic cleaning services, and recreation facilities such as squash courts and outdoor hockey rinks.

Impact and benefit agreements with First Nations communities, a consequence of the Crown's duty to consult and accommodate Indigenous groups when a development will affect them, also decrease the likelihood of a small city arising in the lowlands. As guardians of the Breathing Lands who generally follow the seventh generation principle, the First Nations communities in and around the Ring of Fire will likely insist on a minimal environmental footprint for any development. A lump sum payment and an annual pittance in exchange for the right to pillage and pollute won't cut it in twenty-first-century Canada.

But a few hundred kilometres south of the Ring of Fire, at the beginning of the proposed north-south road to the mining camp, lies the sleepy but sprawling community of Greenstone, population roughly 5,000. Born of an amalgamation of several smaller towns and reserves along Highway 11 (part of the Trans-Canada highway), Greenstone has branded itself the "Gateway to the Ring of Fire."

The former towns within Greenstone owe their existence to the CPR railway, gold, and pulp and paper. Eight mines operated in the area between 1936 and 1970, producing millions of ounces of gold, followed by a thriving pulp and paper industry. Geraldton, the largest of the communities, is the hometown of International Dublin Literary award winner Jane Urquhart and other luminaries. But many of these towns fell into decline when the mines and mills closed. The amalgamated region is struggling.

If the Ring of Fire development and the north-south road from the area proceed, Greenstone would become an important transfer point for supplies and ore going to and from the mines. To add to the economic viability of the region, the Ontario Power Authority is considering a transmission corridor that would supply the Ring of Fire with power and bring grid-connected electricity to the communities in the vicinity of the mines. And in 2021 construction started on a 700-kilometre, long-haul fibre-optic broadband network that will provide high-speed internet access to the fly-in communities of Eabametoong, Nibinamik, Neskantaga, Webequie, and Marten Falls. The provincial and federal governments pledged C$67 million towards the project, which will allow residents to participate more fully in the modern economy. And potentially stem the exodus of youth from their communities.

This holy trinity of infrastructure, natural resources, and government has worked in the past to boost economies in Canada. "During northern Ontario's development, economic growth was most robust during eras where all three engines came together to provide the impetus for economic growth and employment creation," according to economist Livio Di Matteo.[17]

The region could use the jobs. Between 1990 and 2019, northern Ontario experienced employment declines while the rest of the province grew. The northwest, where the Ring of Fire is located, shrank by 7 percent.

Though most of the jobs in the Ring of Fire would go to First Nations community members living closer to the mines, Greenstone might also house miners on rotation. As its population grows, the community could become an important hub for northern Ontario. While perhaps never reaching the vibrant diversification the city of Sudbury has achieved, Greenstone could, on the other hand, follow a less destructive trajectory.

In September 2020, the Minodahmun development company representing First Nations communities near Greenstone, including Aroland, Animbiigoo Zaagi'igan Anishinaabek, and Ginoogaming, launched an employment training program. The Readiness and Essential Skills for Employment Training (RESET) program will train Indigenous people interested in mining and construction to work at developments there and in the Ring of Fire. The first mine to benefit from the program will be Equinox Gold and Orion Mine Finance's Greenstone gold project, a C$1.3-billion open-pit gold mine under construction as of mid-2022.

"The region is set to experience unprecedented growth and investment related to mineral development," said Minodahmun CEO John Glover. "It is crucial that governments and mining companies make an investment in helping to create a strong First Nation workforce in this new Ontario mining hub. This will keep benefits from mineral development in the north and help to address unemployment in First Nations."

It's a start.

PART III

Power and Protest

CHAPTER 9

A Tale of Two Provinces

On Earth Day, 1990, a war canoe sliced through the Hudson River current past the Statue of Liberty, then docked at the heart of New York City. Perched in the bow sporting a bright orange life jacket was Cree Grand Chief Matthew Coon Come, beaming at the cheering crowd gathered in the harbour. The murky waters of the Hudson lapped against the pier as New Yorkers reached out to greet him.

Propelling the boat were Cree and Inuit paddlers. They had just travelled a remarkable 1,642 kilometres as the crow flies in their Odeyak — a combination of "ode," the Cree word for canoe, and "yak," from the Inuit word "kayak." A dogsled team had dragged the eight-metre-long vessel from Kuujjuarapik, Quebec, on the remote eastern shores of Hudson Bay, across the snow and ice to the nearest road. There, a support crew loaded the vessel onto a truck for the long journey south. After a quick stop in Canada's capital, where their demands had fallen on unreceptive ears, the protesters launched their Odeyak into the Ottawa River. They paddled east to Montreal before turning south along the Richelieu and Hudson Rivers, crossing the international border at the village of Rouses Point, New York. Cree and Inuit travelling in buses and accompanying canoes formed a convoy of fellow protesters.

Adorned with paintings of bear and Canada goose, the Odeyak was a symbol of solidarity between the Cree and Inuit united in their resistance to a vast dam about to be built on their territory on the east coast of Hudson Bay in northern Quebec. The two Indigenous groups had conceived of the journey and built the canoe-kayak as a public appeal designed to encourage politicians in New York and New England to cancel their power contracts with Hydro-Québec.

Two years previous, in 1988, New York governor Mario Cuomo and Quebec premier Robert Bourassa had ratified a deal to provide the New York Power Authority with 130 billion kilowatt-hours of electricity over twenty years starting in 1995. To achieve this goal, the provincial power supplier proposed damming the Great Whale River in northern Quebec and flooding several thousand hectares of traditional hunting and fishing grounds. The idea was to eventually divert several large rivers, affecting an ecosystem the size of France.

"I feel like, to put it mildly, a conqueror," Premier Bourassa told director Magnus Isacsson as he described the Great Whale project in the film *Power*.[1] "We are economically conquering the north of Quebec."

The cheerful bowman Matthew Coon Come was no longer smiling by the time he climbed the stage in New York's Times Square, flanked by sixty or so of his fellow protesters. His small frame was lost in his big city blazer, but his clear voice boomed: "If they were to build a dam blocking your rivers in America, near your cities, there would be an outcry. But you know what happens on Indian land? They ask us to move over. Move over, Indian, we are going to build. We're saying this is unacceptable." The crowd of roughly 10,000 roared.

His stunt and subsequent lobbying efforts seemed to have an impact. Two years later, after reviewing Hydro-Québec's proposal, Cuomo cancelled the state power authority's contract. Analysts said Cuomo's review was one of the first in U.S. history to weigh large-scale energy purchases against the value of energy conservation and come out on the side of conservation.[2] Though the decision was couched in economic terms, protesters seized the opportunity to say Cuomo had been swayed by their passionate arguments against hydro development.

Stung by the sudden loss of about US$12 billion in contracts, Hydro-Québec publicly denounced the Cree intervention in the deal and vowed to proceed without New York. But the next Quebec premier to rule the province, Jacques Parizeau, officially abandoned the project in 1994 to rid himself of the albatross growing putrid around his neck.

The failed Great Whale proposal resembled Quebec's first major hydroelectric project. Constructed in the 1970s within the next major watershed south of Great Whale at La Grande River, the dam had flooded 11,500 square kilometres of wilderness, about 11 percent of Quebec's landmass. The massive project had submerged trap lines and stirred up naturally occurring mercury, contaminating both fish stocks and drinking water. When 10,000 caribou drowned in a tributary of La Grande River as a result of a badly timed water release, their bloated carcasses floating across the TV screens of the world, Inuit and Cree outrage grew and spread.

They had a legal leg to stand on. Before announcing the massive La Grande development, Quebec had failed to consult the roughly 18,000 Cree and Inuit living in the area, despite the obvious disruption to their lives and livelihood. Refusing to bow to the demands of Hydro-Québec, the Indigenous groups took their fight to the courts. Their main legal argument was that land transfer agreements signed at the turn of the twentieth century required that any surrender of land rights be negotiated and not just assumed. It took three exhausting years of court battles, but the traditional landholders prevailed.

And so, in 1975, the James Bay and Northern Quebec Agreement was born. The "first modern treaty" set the precedent for major land claims agreements in Canada. The deal allowed the Quebec government to resume construction of hydroelectric dams in certain parts of the James Bay region in exchange for recognizing the rights of the Inuit and certain Cree and Naskapi First Nations there, and committing to paying C$225 million in compensation over twenty years. What they had lost in land and wildlife in the 1970s flooding, Indigenous peoples had gained in groundbreaking autonomy. More importantly, the new treaty set the stage for them to wriggle free of the Indian Act. As a result of court challenges following the James Bay agreement, the Quebec Cree were gradually able to gain control over their local government, including health and education. They spawned a Cree civil service and several Cree-owned businesses.

The agreement to cede land was a Faustian bargain. But it gave the Quebec Cree much more power to resist corporate and government interests they didn't support. In 1995, they may have changed the course of Canadian history by swinging the vote far enough to the "no" side to prevent Quebec from separating from Canada. Just before the referendum on separation, the Cree had held their own vote, overwhelmingly rejecting the notion they should be separated from their brethren because of Quebec's desire for independence. Matthew Coon Come argued the Cree would rather stay on dry land within Canada than risk hopping in a boat with Quebec and abandoning their rights to the ancestral land they had inhabited for 5,000 years, an area of one million square kilometres stretching from James Bay to Labrador. "We Won't Go," screamed a *Montreal Gazette* headline. On October 30, 1995, 50.58 percent of Quebecers voted to stay in Canada. If the Cree had not protested so vehemently and publicly, the vote may well have gone the other way.

By that pivotal moment in Canadian history, Coon Come, the thirty-eight-year-old son of a trapper from the village of Mistissini in northern Quebec, had become one of the most powerful figures in Quebec, the unofficial head of a sovereign state. He lived humbly in a one-room cabin heated by a wood stove, but the majority of Cree considered them their highest leader. They voted him in as grand chief three times in a row. In 2000, he was elected national chief of the Assembly of First Nations. For his advocacy on behalf of Indigenous people, he became an officer of the Order of Canada in 2018.

His childhood had been difficult. Born in 1956, he was sent to a residential school in Moosonee, Ontario, at age six, then transferred to another school near Lac St-Jean, Quebec, for several more years. He eventually ended up at a high school in Hull, Quebec. While working towards his secondary school diploma, he found out that his hometown of Mistissini could be flooded if Hydro-Québec's first major hydroelectric development, the aforementioned La Grande project, were to go ahead. He decided he must prevent the dam project if he could.

To that end, he studied political science at Trent University in Ontario. He was about to begin McGill University's law program in Montreal when he was called back to Mistissini to run for deputy chief of the village. At the age of twenty-one, Coon Come became one of the youngest Cree elected officials, and by 1987 he was the grand chief of the Cree Nation. While he was too late to prevent La Grande, he and his team hatched the plan to paddle to New York City in 1990 when Hydro-Québec was threatening to flood even more Cree land with its Great Whale project.

But even with the Great Whale win and Quebec's decision to remain within Canada — both huge milestones for the Quebec Cree — the rights fight was far from over. In July 1998, frustrated by several breaches of the James Bay agreement, the region's Indigenous peoples launched a lawsuit against the Quebec government demanding full compliance with the agreement, revenue sharing, and more say over natural resource exploitation, preservation of their trap lines, and a cessation of clear-cutting. Once more, they were victorious. And growing increasingly powerful on the national stage.

In what lawyer and treaty negotiator Bill Gallagher called "a remarkable judicial outcome,"[3] the Supreme Court of Canada's ruling that Quebec's secession would violate constitutional law specified that Indigenous land position had to be recognized in any reformulation of Quebec's boundaries. The ruling muted any further grumbles by Quebec separatists who longed to create the boundaries of an independent Quebec.

"The Crees' derailment of the Great Whale project signalled the stark reality that Quebec's hydropower options were becoming increasingly limited," Gallagher wrote in *Resource Rulers: Fortune and Folly on Canada's Road to Resources*. "In addition, the secession reference signalled that natives [sic] were largely in the driver's seat when it came to re-drawing the map of Quebec."

※

The promise of snow was in the air on March 8, 1998, when Newfoundland premier Brian Tobin fled from the back seat of the vehicle ferrying him through a silent grey day in Labrador. At least he had thought to wear his sealskin coat. Grasping Tobin's arm, eyes downcast, shivering in his thin wool coat and further supported by a cane in his free hand was fifty-nine-year-old Quebec premier Lucien Bouchard.[4] Bouchard had developed necrotizing fasciitis and had had his leg amputated to stop the flesh-eating disease. His consequent limp was slowing him down.

The two premiers had set out triumphantly that day. They'd notified the national media they would be officially launching a new hydroelectric development at Churchill Falls, Labrador, in the small town named after the powerful cataract. The event would celebrate the end of a twenty-five-year impasse between the two provinces and the beginning of a new deal that would guarantee Newfoundland and Labrador's access to transmission lines powered by a new generating station at the existing Churchill Falls site.

Things didn't quite work out that way. Instead, their motorcade was met by a crowd of 100 angry protesters blocking the road into town. Still seeking compensation for the flooding that occurred when the first Churchill dam was built in 1971, the Innu — perhaps inspired by their Cree neighbours — weren't about to cave to provincial deals. They used the event to turn the publicity tables. Waving placards that read "No Dam Way" and "Hydro Is a No Go without Innu consent," they shouted "go home" to the politicians.

Bouchard and Tobin escaped the crowd by leaping out of their vehicle and scurrying arm in arm along the icy road to a helicopter summoned to rescue them. A new venue was hastily arranged to salvage the press conference, but the protesters persisted. The premiers finally gave up and retreated to their respective thrones in Quebec City and St. John's.

The Churchill Falls expansion had met the same fate as the Great Whale project. It was a royal embarrassment, a colossal misread of the zeitgeist. More importantly, the failed government ambition confirmed, once again, that Indigenous land rights in Canada could not be ignored when it came to resource development.

✳

The Quebec Cree's struggle to be accommodated culminated in a 2002 deal with the province called the Paix des Braves, a nation-to-nation agreement to partner on economic and community development for the next fifty years. The agreement gave the Cree C\$3.5 billion over the span of the contract and stipulated that the Quebec government and the Cree should jointly manage Cree lands and share in any benefits from natural resources, including forestry, hydroelectric projects, and mining.

In 2011, for instance, the owners of the Éléonore gold mine (now owned and operated by Denver-based Newmont, the world's largest gold mining company), the Cree Nation of Wemindji, the Grand Council of the Crees (Eeyou Istchee), and the Cree Regional Authority signed a collaboration agreement to protect Cree traditional activities, operate the gold mine in a sustainable manner, and ensure the Cree benefit from employment, business, and training programs. There are about 350 Cree from Wemindji — 400 kilometres away by road and 200 kilometres by plane — working at the mine, and hundreds of millions of dollars of construction and service contracts have been awarded to various Cree businesses over the years since Éléonore was built.

In the span of a few decades, the Quebec Cree have gone from impoverished, powerless, and poorly organized residents of northern Quebec to a powerful Nation with autonomy, successful businesses, and legal wins on their side. They still grapple with poor housing and health problems such as diabetes, but they are considerably more comfortable than their relatives just across the bay in Ontario, who have had nothing on the scale of the Hydro-Québec projects to use for leverage. Although De Beers was secretly searching for diamonds on lands the Ontario Cree and Ojibway had inhabited for centuries at about the same time the Quebec Cree were signing their landmark land claims agreement, it would be decades before De Beers built the Victor diamond mine there. Even then, the project was small relative to the Quebec hydroelectric dams, and benefits to the community were questionable.

In late April 2016, a Cree-owned Air Creebec plane landed in Attawapiskat. The plane carried letters and artwork of support from the Quebec Cree in Wemindji across the bay from their sister community in Ontario, where suicide, lack of potable water, and inadequate housing have become a part of everyday life. Denis Georgekish, chief of Wemindji, told the *National Post*: "Our hearts go out to them. They're Crees like us. Even if there's water dividing us, we're still the same people."[5]

CHAPTER 10

From Backrooms to Bulldozers

The sun reflects off snow left over from last night's storm, blinding me as I ascend in a cloud of steam from Toronto's Osgoode subway station to the sub-zero air at street level.

I'm on my way to visit former Ontario premier Bob Rae, chief negotiator for the Matawa Tribal Council for five years until 2018, when the Conservative premier Doug Ford was elected and the province cancelled funding for talks on the Ring of Fire. Rae remains an advisor to First Nations communities near the Ring of Fire. But the days when a deal to develop the mineral deposits seemed in his grasp are over.

It's Friday, December 20, 2019, and half the city appears to have cleared out for Christmas vacation. I've managed to avoid the forced intimacy of the usual subway commute. And if I aimed carefully enough, I could shoot a puck down the normally crowded sidewalk of Toronto's University Avenue without bruising anyone's ankle.

But the offices of Olthuis, Kleer, Townshend, a law firm that advocates for Indigenous and treaty rights nationwide, are humming. Some of the younger staff are regrouping at the reception desk after flying in from meeting with clients in Thunder Bay, Ontario, and Medicine Hat, Alberta, both communities with large First Nations representation. They have stories to tell each other. I do my best not to eavesdrop.

Senior Counsel Rae — whose daughter Judith Rae is a partner in the firm — emerges from his office precisely at 10 a.m., our appointed meeting time. I'm surprised by how grateful I am for this gesture of punctuality so rarely afforded to members of the media anymore. But just as I stand to greet Rae, he instructs me to sit back down and maybe find a cup of coffee because there's an unexpected call coming in from a government minister. Mildly deflated, I pick up a copy of *Uphere*, "the voice of Canada's north," from a selection of magazines on the coffee table. The publications seem like artifacts from an age when people still read print media for information and entertainment.

I quickly find myself engrossed in an article that references a book by Patrick White,[1] a *Globe and Mail* reporter, about an RCMP officer who lived among the Inuit. White has some regrets about how he's covered the North and its people, fearing he may have come across as some kind of expert when in reality he'd only spent a short time there: "You spend a day in the Arctic, you've got a newspaper article; a week, you've got a magazine article; you spend a month, you're entitled to write an entire book once you get back."[2] He's paraphrasing author Ernie Lyall, who worked on the front lines for the Hudson's Bay Company in the early part of the twentieth century building stores and establishing trading partnerships with Indigenous communities in the North. It seemed like a prescient message; I was in the earliest stages of researching this book and unsure about how I would include Indigenous voices from the Ring of Fire region.

Half an hour later, Rae returns with a second apology. I reach to shake his hand, but he's nursing a cold so offers me a friendly fist bump instead. The coronavirus pandemic is still a couple of months from erupting in Canada, but we have an inkling it's coming. He leads me down the lobby area past a wall of Indigenous art and ushers me into a glassed-in boardroom overlooking University Avenue. He takes the chair at the head of the board table, and I sit at a right angle to him, the sun dappling my notebook. Things are looking up.

But before I can even unfold my list of questions, Rae launches into a lecture on the evolution of Indigenous rights in Canada and Ontario's Treaty 9 in particular. I'm reminded that I am talking to a former provincial premier with years of experience dealing with the media. I begin to understand that it is not going to be easy to take the lead in this interview. Over the next hour or so, we wrestle for position — Rae keen to explain legal history, while I try to tease out stories of his time as the chief negotiator for the Matawa Tribal Council. He wins.

I had been planning to travel to the Ring of Fire communities myself for research, but the COVID-19 outbreak that closed off vulnerable First Nations stymied that plan. And while Rae is reluctant to divulge personal experiences in the Far North, citing client privilege, as a former provincial premier he has valuable perspective on the evolution of the province's approach to the Ring of Fire since Noront's drill first hit the motherlode.

※

Dalton McGuinty was Ontario premier in 2007 when the Ring of Fire was discovered. At the time, the courts were starting to consistently side with First Nations across Canada over the right to be consulted about development on their traditional lands. The province was clumsily playing catch-up.

Ontario's inability to manage disputes between resource developers and First Nations asserting their legal right to consultation — which often involves coordination among several different ministries — culminated in 2008 when Justice Patrick Smith imprisoned Chief Donny Morris and five other members of the Kitchenuhmaykoosib Inninuwug (KI) First Nation for contempt of court. Morris and other community members had been fighting for a decade to stop Platinex Resources from drilling for platinum on KI's traditional lands 600 kilometres north of Thunder Bay, just northwest of the Ring of Fire. Platinex fought back, suing the KI First Nation and the Ontario government for disrupting exploration on claims it had legitimately staked and explored under the Ontario Mining Act.

The case went to the Ontario Court of Appeal, which ruled that the six-month jail sentences meted out by Justice Smith were too harsh. The appeal court reduced them to the ten weeks of time served. Ontario then settled with Platinex, paying C$5 million for losses the company incurred. McGuinty's Liberals withdrew the disputed lands from staking and reformed the Mining Act to include a new vehicle for dispute resolution.

After the verdict, Vernon Morris, chief of the Oji-Cree Muskrat Dam First Nation, stated: "The government's view of duty to consult is that there will be basis for discussions to begin for planning and development.

Our interpretation of the duty to consult is that we have a right to say 'No' when the actions for development will have a harmful effect or no benefit to our First Nation."

It was a watershed case in Ontario, whose provincial leaders would be wary of shirking their duty to consult in the future.

But Dalton McGuinty didn't have much to say about what was happening on the ground in the Ring of Fire until 2010, when Cleveland-based Cliffs Natural Resources started pouring millions of dollars into the area in the hopes of accessing a chromite source to complement its well-established iron ore and steel business. The premier was encouraged by Cliffs' investment and saw the Ring of Fire as an opportunity for Ontario to recover from the 2008–09 global financial crisis. He leaned on the federal government to help build the infrastructure required to get the mines built as quickly as possible.

Up until then, a lot of the Ring of Fire exploration and infrastructure planning had been proceeding without Indigenous consultation, contrary to the growing tendency for the Supreme Court of Canada to rule on the side of First Nations in battles with provinces over resource development. Though most Ontarians were oblivious to the transgressions, the exploration activity did not go unnoticed by Indigenous communities.

Predictably enough, in early 2010, band members of Marten Falls, 100 kilometres southeast of the Ring of Fire, erected a blockade to prevent companies from landing their bush planes on frozen airstrips on Koper Lake and McFaulds Lake, within the community's traditional lands. Without access to the lakes, Noront, Cliffs, and other companies would be unable to fly in supplies and personnel to conduct what they considered vital winter exploration in the region.

Led by Chief Elias Moonias, Marten Falls established the blockades not necessarily because the community members wanted to prevent further exploration, but because they wanted the companies to use their airstrip and their winter road instead of the frozen lakes. "We are not against mining and want to do business, but we want to do it together," Chief Moonias told the Canadian Press.[3]

To calm the waters, McGuinty sent Northern Development and Mines Minister Michael Gravelle to Marten Falls to find out how to appease community members. Minister Gravelle met with Chief Moonias, hammered out an agreement, then dined on moose stew with the rest of the community before hopping on a puddle jumper to fly to Webequie, west of the potential mine sites.[4]

Under the agreement, Marten Falls agreed to lift the blockades in exchange for the Ontario government hearing out the demands of Moonias and Webequie Chief Cornelius Wabasse. If the chiefs were not satisfied with the negotiations over demands for a revamped airport, environmental impact reviews, training and job guarantees, an extended road network, and a better memorandum of understanding with the government, they would resume the blockade. But resolving the conflict was never going to be that easy. While Gravelle feasted on stew and exchanged gifts with Moonias, some of the community's youth stood silently on the fringes of the gathering with placards reading "This land is our land."

In 2011 the province stepped up its commitment to the process by creating a Ring of Fire Secretariat, essentially a new government department to encourage development of the chromite and other deposits while taking into account environmental impacts and the economic needs of the First Nations communities.

At a Ring of Fire infrastructure conference held in Thunder Bay in mid-2011, Gravelle outlined the extraordinary, once-in-a-century opportunity the Ring of Fire represented. "We need to get it right, that is why we have set up a Ring of Fire coordinator, why we are setting up a Ring of Fire Secretariat, and why we are working so hard with all the partners, the First Nations and the companies, to make sure we move forward together," he said. "That is crucially important."[5]

But the next year, McGuinty — the first Liberal premier to secure three consecutive terms in office since the nineteenth century — was forced to step down amid indignation over what was considered a scandalous decision to cancel gas-powered electrical plants in NIMBY Liberal ridings at a cost to taxpayers of C$1 billion.

Kathleen Wynne succeeded McGuinty. She too considered the Ring of Fire a unique opportunity to satisfy northern constituents, advance Indigenous reconciliation, and fill government coffers. Her approach was more conciliatory.

She set up a meeting with the Matawa Tribal Council of nine First Nations, the first the council had had with a sitting premier since 1975.

By the time they parted ways, Wynne and the council had established the basic pillars of a framework agreement for development of the Ring of Fire: employment and training opportunities; effective land management that respects environmental protection; resource revenue sharing; and infrastructure where there was none.

The new premier moved quickly to set the negotiations in motion. She appointed retired Supreme Court justice Frank Iacobucci to serve as chief negotiator for the province. Bob Rae stepped in as chief negotiator on behalf of the Matawa Tribal Council. Optimism was in the air.

"My job arose out of the First Nations' desire to engage with the provincial and federal governments in a more collective way because Cliffs' proposed mine was a huge development that would have a wide impact," said Rae. "We did have the attention of the premier and she met openly with us. The chiefs didn't like everything they heard because she was telling it as she saw it as first minister. But she really paid attention."

Still, the legacy of distrust established over the decades the Crown had repeatedly failed to meet its treaty obligations to First Nations remained a dark cloud over the negotiations. And Cliffs, beginning to suffer financially, was growing impatient with the endless meetings between government, Indigenous groups, and industry in Toronto and Thunder Bay that never seemed to resolve anything.

"If a company shows up with a bag of money, surely you find a way to help them spend it," said David Anthony, former VP and senior project director for Cliffs, who quit the project in frustration in 2012. "I think if you go to fifteen different meetings and no progress is made, you come to the conclusion that [development] is never going to happen."

Exacerbating the dysfunction was an assumption that all nine of the First Nations of the Matawa Tribal Council would speak with a common voice. The council's slogan is "The Power of Unity. The Dignity of Difference." While the communities are united in their belief that they have jurisdiction over their traditional lands, the Ring of Fire discussions only served to emphasize their differences. Four of the communities (Aroland, Constance Lake, Ginoogaming, and Long Lake #58) have access to all-season roads; the other five (Eabametoong, Nibinamik, Neskantaga, Marten Falls, and Webequie) are only accessible by air or winter road, so their priorities regarding infrastructure are different. Marten Falls,

Webequie, Neskantaga, and Nibinamik are the closest communities to the proposed development and have the most to gain from jobs and training programs, but Neskantaga also lies on the shores of Attawapiskat Lake, an important and relatively pristine source of fish that could be disrupted by mining activity or road building.

And nothing about the formation and evolution of the nine communities had been organic. "The political structures and how they express themselves are a consequence of the Indian Act," said Rae. "When people say, 'Why can't you just agree?' they respond, 'Well, why did you create nine communities to represent a few thousand people?' The communities are different because a lot of things have happened historically to create different dynamics," including abuse suffered at the hands of priests visiting the communities to convert their members to Christianity. The resulting trauma, and disagreements about how to respond to the church, divided clans and families. The Nations found it difficult to reach consensus on all the issues that confronted them.

Meanwhile, shaken by lower commodity prices and an erosion of shareholder confidence, Cliffs was getting cold feet as the negotiations dragged on. Finally, after spending about C$550 million in the region over four years, the company announced it was pulling out of the project in late 2013. Its new CEO, Lourenco Goncalves, who was parachuted in to revive the American company's flagging fortunes, went so far as to say the Ring of Fire was beyond the point of no return.

Cliffs' departure was unsurprising given the company's internal turmoil coupled with the uncertainty surrounding the Ring of Fire, and with Cliffs went the urgency to strike a deal with the First Nations. All that was left in the Ring of Fire was a handful of junior companies without the financial resources to achieve much more than a little grassroots exploration. It seemed like a death knell for the ambitious development project.

"I did not once hear the Ontario government say [they were] ready to fund a road. It was always: let's get together for lunch, we'll pay a bunch of people to come to the meeting, we'll go over the same stuff we've gone over a hundred times before. And at the end of the meeting, there will not be a single resolution or any indication that we actually plan to do something," David Anthony told me. "If [they] had said they would build a road and toll it back to us, or at least start a dialogue about how a road could get built, there might be a whole chromite industry in Canada right now."

But the province was undeterred. In mid-2014, Premier Wynne announced that her minority government was prepared to contribute C$1 billion to build a road to the Ring of Fire. Minister Gravelle implored the federal government to match the infrastructure funds, calling the Ring of Fire a "project of national significance." He wrote to his counterpart in Ottawa, Greg Rickford, requesting a meeting "at your earliest convenience to discuss the [Ring of Fire] and the importance of a strong federal role in ensuring this development can proceed and its economic benefits for Ontario, First Nations and Canada can be realized."[6]

But the feds, then led by Conservative prime minister Stephen Harper, were mostly silent on the file. They said they would need a detailed plan from Ontario, including fully costed infrastructure proposals, before they would be willing to step into the fray. Part of the challenge was that Indigenous affairs are handled federally, while mining falls under provincial jurisdiction. Rarely do the two levels of government confer on those two areas of interest. It's a convenient means to dodge the issue.

At a meeting in Timmins in March 2015, federal Treasury Board President Tony Clement reiterated that the Ring of Fire needed two things before the federal government would take a sustained interest: a worthwhile return on investment and a good working relationship between the province and the First Nations. In his opinion, the proposed development lacked both.

The dismissal by the federal government was frustrating not only for the province but also for the First Nations involved. Canada has certain obligations to Indigenous peoples recognized and affirmed in section 35 of the Constitution Act, 1982, interpreted to include a wide of range of cultural, economic, and political rights.[7] The Matawa Tribal Council rightly expected, at the very least, to have discussions with representatives in Ottawa, not just be left at the mercy of the province.

Eventually, Wynne herself grew impatient with the impasse. She sent a letter to the Council Chiefs in May 2017, demanding that they come together on decisions or she would scrap the regional framework and deal with the communities on an individual basis. In her letter, Wynne told the chiefs they "should not squander" her 2014 commitment to spend C$1 billion to help build a road to the deposits in the Ring of Fire.[8]

"We have not achieved much of the progress on road and infrastructure development that we had hoped for under the RFA [regional framework agreement] over the past three years," Wynne wrote in the letter. "While I continue to hope progress can be made, I am prepared to continue to advance discussions with those First Nations that would like to pursue transportation infrastructure through our bilateral process."

After many months at the negotiating table, Rae was equally discouraged. "Frustrating is not a strong enough word. There was a moment in time when we had a framework worked out and signed and the provincial government was willing to make some investment in the communities and their well-being," he said. "But there was not enough trust on the table for [the communities] to move ahead."

Neskantaga was particularly wary. While Chief Wayne Moonias believed Wynne's heart was in the right place and she understood the suffering the First Nation had endured under Treaty 9, he said it was "disingenuous" of her to expect Indigenous peoples to cooperate with resource permits on their land while their own jurisdictional claims went unaddressed.[9]

Tensions escalated when the province signed agreements with Webequie and Marten Falls to make them proponents on the environmental assessments to build roads into their communities (from the Ring of Fire in Webequie's case and from a forestry road that leads to the town of Nakina in Marten Falls' case).

The neighbouring communities of Neskantaga and Eabametoong viewed the decision as favouritism and accused the Wynne government of acting in bad faith by not adhering to the regional framework agreement. They considered the agreements an attempt to "divide and conquer" the First Nations within the Matawa Tribal Council.[10]

"The approach the Wynne government is taking to roads in the Ring of Fire is a scandal and could be a nail in the coffin for our Aboriginal rights and way of life," the two communities said in a joint media release issued in May 2018.

A month later, Wynne was voted out of office and replaced as premier by Conservative Doug Ford. At least Wynne was the devil they knew.

*

"If I have to hop on that bulldozer myself with Vic [Nipissing MPP Vic Fedeli] on the other one, we're going to start building the roads to get to the mining," Ford announced in the lead-up to the election as he outlined the Conservative Party's plans for Ontario's Far North, including the Ring of Fire.

One could almost hear the cries of frustration coming from some of the Matawa chiefs more than 1,000 kilometres to the north. After getting so close to a negotiated agreement with the provincial government to develop the Ring of Fire, it seemed as if their voices would dissipate in the vast swamp. The divide and conquer mentality would prevail.

During his campaign, Doug Ford was best known as the brother of disgraced former Toronto mayor Rob Ford. Almost no one in Toronto expected "Dougie" to win the premiership. But the populist was beloved by "Ford Nation," supporters mostly from rural areas and the suburbs. That demographic, and a growing unease with Wynne's policies among the general population, was enough to put "Trump Light" — as Ford was labelled — in the premier's seat. But even though he branded himself as the working man's premier, Ford could never presume to speak for the North, with its unique population of Indigenous people and unionized workers who tended to lean left. The federal riding of Timmins–James Bay has been held by NDP MP Charlie Angus for almost two decades.

Ford insisted on doing so anyway.

Once he became premier, he pledged to cut "red tape and restrictions that are blocking important economic developments" in the Ring of Fire and other parts of northern Ontario. He slashed the provincial budget for Indigenous affairs, responsible for promoting collaboration across ministries in partnership with Indigenous communities. He scrapped the regional framework agreement and vowed to talk to each First Nation separately on the projects or roads that would affect their communities directly.

"The problem with that approach," said Rae, "is that all the other communities are saying, 'We have rights too.' You are setting the cat among the pigeons."

Opposition New Democrats' Indigenous Affairs critic and Kiiwetinoong MPP Sol Mamakwa agreed. He expressed concern that one-on-one agreements could be used to pit individual First Nations against one another as feared. On the other hand, "the regional framework agreement provided a process of dialogue [for] First Nations and, not only that, it . . . gave communities a process to work together."[11]

Aside from infuriating many of the First Nations, all these bold promises to get development going rang hollow to another vital stakeholder group in the Ring of Fire's inner circle: the investors expected to provide the financing for the mines. From June 2018, when Ford was elected premier, to the end of 2019, the value of Noront — the main player in the Ring of Fire — dropped by 50 percent to 21 cents per share. Investors knew that, given the complications, developing mines there was going to be a potentially insurmountable challenge.

Meanwhile, the First Nations in the region continued to win in the courts. In July 2018, a three-judge panel of the Divisional Court of Ontario's Superior Court of Justice cancelled permits issued to Landore Resources Canada to explore lands near Eabametoong. Although the judges considered the duty to consult in this case to be "at the lower end of the spectrum," because the land had been surrendered to the Crown under Treaty 9 and the proposed exploration was minimally disruptive, they upheld that duty based on precedent.

Krista Robertson, the lawyer for Eabametoong, said at the time, "Disingenuous consultation is epidemic across Canada. . . . First Nations constantly feel betrayed by it."[12]

We've been chatting for over an hour when Rae begins to jiggle the change in his pocket impatiently. He admits he is anxious to move on to other business before the firm closes for the Christmas holidays. As we agree to wrap up the interview, he leaves me with a parting thought: "Good public policy is what happens when you've exhausted all the alternatives. Maybe it just wasn't the right moment. We'll have to figure out when that moment is and what it takes to get there."

CHAPTER 11

Circus Acts

In May 2011, the Wildlands League sent a letter to Canada's minister of the environment, Peter Kent, calling for a regional assessment of the Ring of Fire. An Ontario NGO that promotes responsible use of provincial resources, the league emphasized the importance of evaluating the long-term and cumulative environmental impacts of mining before Cliffs, the American miner, mobilized any bulldozers.

As the letter pointed out, among other environmental considerations, "about a tenth of the globe's cooling benefit from peatlands comes from Ontario's Hudson Bay Lowlands."[1]

At first, the response from the feds seemed promising. "Given that the project is sited in the upper reaches of several major watersheds which outlet to the highly sensitive and ecologically important James Bay and Hudson Bay coastal ecosystems, the potential for cumulative effects to occur outside of the project . . . needs to be considered," Environment Canada advised the Canadian Environmental Assessment Agency in a memo. "The cumulative effects of known and anticipated mining and other developments on Ontario's Far North could be substantial if not sufficiently understood and managed at the regional scale."[2]

First Nations communities near and downstream of the proposed development echoed the call for a comprehensive assessment of the area by way of a joint review panel, an environmental assessment completed by the federal government and provincial governments together to avoid duplication. Even Noront requested a regional land use plan from one or both levels of government to inject some certainty into its own planning.

While the feds sat on their hands, members of the Ontario government were touring the province touting the economic potential of the Ring of Fire. They cited a back-of-the-envelope guess by the former chief scientist for the Geological Society of Canada, Jim Franklin, as if it were a fully costed absolute, that the value of the rocks in the ground could be worth C$60 billion.

They rarely mentioned potential environmental or social impacts.

In September 2011 Liberal leader Dalton McGuinty called the Ring "the most promising mining opportunity in Canada in a century."[3] Progressive Conservative leader Tim Hudak went even further, saying that "in many ways, the Ring of Fire is Ontario's oil sands — an enormous wealth beneath the earth that can break open a new frontier for job creation and investment in our province. Sometimes we look with wonder and awe at what Alberta can do; we can do that in Ontario and we can do that with the Ring of Fire."

When Cliffs pulled the plug in 2013, the feds fell silent. One could imagine entire government departments in Ottawa breathing a collective sigh of relief that the complicated Ring of Fire file would no longer be their responsibility.

The calendar flipped forward. Half a dozen years passed. Cliffs sold its mining claims in the Ring of Fire to Noront for a pittance. Frank Iacobucci and Bob Rae tried and failed to negotiate a deal between the province and the Matawa Tribal Council for development. Government officials and provincial premiers came and went.

Then, in 2019, Canada introduced a new Impact Assessment Act aimed at streamlining the approvals process for natural resource projects, while improving consultation with Indigenous peoples. The new legislation took a more holistic approach to assessment by evaluating not just environmental impacts but the effect of the projects on local economies, human health, and community.

The Ring of Fire was an obvious candidate for the type of comprehensive regional assessment now outlined in the act, which so many had called for when exploration was first ramping up.

Simplified geology map showing the McFaulds Lake greenstone belt (Ring of Fire). Green represents the volcanic belt; yellows and pinks are granitic rocks; blue represents mafic (dark igneous) intrusive rocks. D.R.B. Rainsford., P.A. Diorio, R.L.S. Hogg, and R.T. Metsaranta, "The Use of Geophysics in the Ring of Fire, James Bay Lowlands — The Chromite Story," in V. Tschirhart and M.D. Thomas (eds.), *Proceedings of Exploration 17: Sixth Decennial International Conference on Mineral Exploration*, pp. 649–662 (2017).

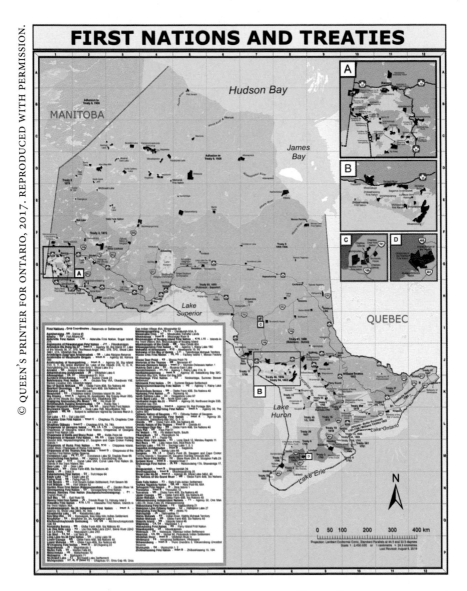

Ontario First Nations and treaties, 2019. The blue and mauve areas north of the Great Lakes watershed represent Treaty 9 and encompass the Ring of Fire. Sudbury falls within Treaty 61, also known as the Robinson-Huron Treaty.

Cree hunting/fishing camp on James Bay near Fort Albany, August 1963.

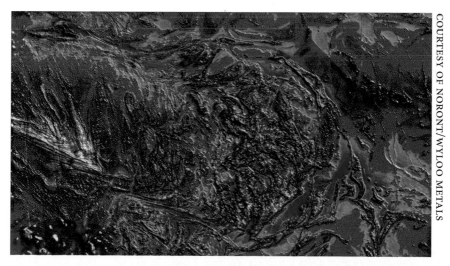

The airborne magnetometer survey clearly shows the Ring of Fire as a magnetic high created by iron-rich rocks in the shape of a semicircle 60 kilometres in diameter.

Chief Monias — Fort Hope. Lake Eambamet

Chief [Moonias] waiting for the Treaty 9 signing ceremony, Fort Hope (Eabametoong), July 19, 1905.

A group of children at a Native residential school in Moose Factory, ca. 1915. Children from the lowlands First Nations were forced to board at schools far from home.

As part of the consultation process, Noront staff show Webequie First Nation leaders geophysical maps and drill core from the Ring of Fire. From left to right: Chief Cornelius Wabasse, Alec Wabasse, and Roy Spence.

From left to right: Greg Rickford, Minister of Energy, Northern Development and Mines, poses for a photo with Chief Bruce Achneepineskum of Marten Falls First Nation and Chief Cornelius Wabasse of Webequie First Nation at the PDAC 2020 Convention.

From left to right: Richard Nemis with his father, James Nemis, founder of Noront Steel, and brother Terry Nemis, who went on to become president of Noront Steel.

Richard Nemis loved to fish in the lakes of northern Ontario.

Richard Nemis managed to tie up a lot of ground for Noront during the early days of the Ring of Fire staking rush.

A square metre of peatland in the Hudson Bay and James Bay Lowlands contains about five times the amount of carbon as one square metre of tropical rainforest in the Amazon.

Getting ready for drilling.

Setting up drills in the bog is a challenge.

With no roads in the region, explorers rely heavily on expensive helicopter support.

A typical shoreline in the James Bay Lowlands.

Setting up the transmitter and receiver loop for a VTEM (Versatile Time Domain Electromagnetic) airborne geophysical survey.

Esker exploration crew, 2021. From left to right: Mike Desilets, Geoff Heggie, Barb Wilson, Steve Pigeon, Archie Moonias, Dwight Shewaybick, Keaton Markham, Steve Sagutch, and Olivia Lachaine.

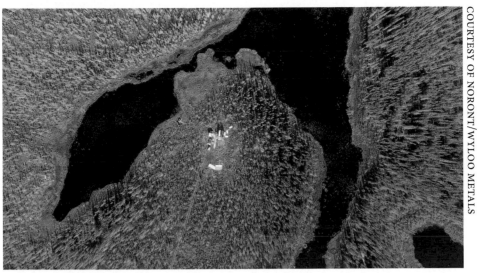

Drill site within Noront's Ring of Fire claim holdings.

Esker exploration camp.

Airstrip on a frozen lake near the Ring of Fire.

Esker exploration camp in winter.

Picking up the loop wire for the geophysical survey.

Esker crew, 2017. From left to right: Geoff Heggie, Elias Whitehead, Dave Ritch, Kaitlyn Paiement, Rob Mitchell, Troy Major, Norma Achneepineskum, Matt Deller, Ryan Weston, and Ralph MacNally.

Helicopter awaits the next day's work.

Moving the drill core out for lab testing.

Neil Novak shows the drill core from the Big Daddy chromite deposit to a visiting geologist in autumn 2009.

Winners of the PDAC Bill Dennis Prospector of the Year Award, 2010. From left to right: Ed Thompson (PDAC), Mac Watson, Richard Nemis, John Harvey, Donald Hoy, and Neil Novak.

Me paddling the Missinaibi River, July 2020.

In early 2020, the federal minister of Environment and Climate Change, Jonathan Wilkinson, ordered just that, reasoning that mining in the Ring of Fire could also cause adverse effects within federal jurisdiction, including on climate change, fish habitat, and migratory bird populations. The project was back on the federal front burner.

Even so, some of the First Nations in the region — Attawapiskat, Fort Albany, and Kashechewan on the James Bay coast and Eabametoong and Neskantaga in the interior — objected to this new approach and its terms of reference (TOR). In a letter to the new federal environment minister Steven Guilbeault early in 2022, these Nations stated, "Your draft TOR is narrow in geographic and activity scope, and wrongly excludes us Indigenous peoples from all but token roles."[4] They called for a true partnership and decision-making powers in the assessment.

Exacerbating their frustration was a provincial government that resisted a regional approach, preferring instead to support infrastructure building and mine development on a project-by-project basis.

❋

On June 25, 2007, several members of Grassy Narrows First Nation gathered on the front lawn of Queen's Park. They'd just walked 1,850 kilometres from Kenora to Toronto, the equivalent of forty-four marathons. Joining them were members of the Kitchenuhmaykoosib Inninuwug (KI) and Ardoch Algonquin First Nations and other Indigenous leaders from across Ontario. They were protesting mineral exploration on their lands in Ontario and calling for the release of Algonquin leader Robert Lovelace and six other KI First Nation leaders. Lovelace had been sentenced to six months in jail for protesting uranium exploration on traditional land around Sharbot Lake north of Kingston. The KI leaders had received equal sentences for contempt of court after violating an injunction to protest the Platinex drilling on their traditional territory.

The Queen's Park gathering was the culmination of protests that had been building momentum as many Ontarians, with the support of luminaries such as Margaret Atwood and Stephen Lewis, called out the unfairness of the Indigenous leaders' incarceration and demanded their release.

The pressure prompted Premier Dalton McGuinty to finally dust off the ancient provincial Mining Act and make some changes. Mining was no longer the only game in town in the North anyway. Instead, the sector competed with other land uses, including forestry, recreation, and conservation.

"The Mining Act, as it is currently written, is not in keeping with our standards and expectations and values that we share today," McGuinty conceded after one of the protest rallies in Toronto.

The Ontario Mining Act of 1873 was designed to encourage exploration and promote settlement in the North, where most of the province's mineral deposits are located. The thinking was that mining could become the cornerstone of development in northern Ontario, creating wealth and tax revenue for the region and the province. The plan succeeded — some would say too well.

The Sudbury nickel-copper deposits discovered in a railway cut at the end of the nineteenth century have by now produced a gross metal value of more than C$500 billion. Not long after the Sudbury basin discoveries, the rich silver mines of Cobalt, Ontario, were uncovered, allowing a new stock exchange to flourish and eventually establish itself on Bay Street to become what's now known as the Toronto Stock Exchange. The Cobalt prospectors, in turn, spread northwest to Timmins, where they discovered the Porcupine gold deposits. Those have produced another US$200 billion or so of gold (at 2022 prices).

And so on and so on. By 2019, mining was directly contributing about C$10 billion to Ontario's economy annually. Ontario had become the top jurisdiction for mineral production in Canada, and one of the top jurisdictions in the world. Communities such as Timmins, Kirkland Lake, Red Lake, and Hemlo had sprung up throughout the North and become self-sustaining.

A lot of men became extremely rich in the process: Harry Oakes, considered among the wealthiest in the colonies when he was murdered in the 1943, made his fortune in the Kirkland Lake Gold Camp; Benny Hollinger, a former barber who discovered some of the richest Porcupine gold deposits, had a massive gold mine named after him; Noah Timmins and his brother Henry, who struck it rich in the Cobalt silver camp, went on to develop the Timmins gold camp; and Thayer Lindsley, born in Japan to American parents, established the massive Falconbridge mining enterprise after purchasing mineral claims near Sudbury. Meanwhile, traditional Indigenous hunting and fishing grounds were destroyed by the disturbance and pollution the mines generated, the treaties negotiated with the settlers either ignored or misinterpreted.

It took several years to hammer out the details, but in 2012 the province unveiled a new Ontario Mining Act. The amended regulations upped the expectations for consultation with Indigenous peoples from the earliest stages of mineral exploration. Prospectors could no longer just stake a claim and get to work. Instead, they were required to submit plans for low-impact exploration, such as mapping, and apply for permits for higher-impact activities, such as drilling. Indigenous communities were to be consulted on all plans and permits before the provincial government made a decision to reject or accept them, sometimes with conditions attached. The consultation process was absolutely key to winning Indigenous support for any exploration or mining activity on their traditional territories.

Later, the province established an online registration system for mining claims based on a latitudinal and longitudinal grid, rather than the ground and map-staking systems that had been in place for more than a century. The Ontario Mineral Tenure Grid now splits the province up into more than 5.2 million cells, ranging in size from 17.7 hectares in the north to 24 hectares in the south.

As the province was tinkering with mining legislation, Ontario's Far North Act (FNA) was written into law to encourage community-based land use planning. The Far North covers 42 percent of Ontario. About 90 percent of the population is Indigenous. The act aimed to protect half of the boreal wilderness of about 225,000 square kilometres, while at the same "partnering" with First Nations on decision-making and revenue sharing from mining and other commercial activities.

While the FNA was hailed as an ecological victory by urban environmentalists, the First Nations who actually live in the Far North felt completely sidelined. Under the act, they could be forced to set aside some of their land for protection regardless of whether they wanted to: the opposite of consultation.

According to Nishwawbe Aski Nation (NAN) Grand Chief Alvin Fiddler, who presided over forty-five Nations under Treaties 9 and 5 from

2015 to 2021, "Ontario does not have free rein to do as it pleases in the Far North, and we will defend our right to control development so that the wealth from our lands benefits our people and the growth of our Nation. We welcome the opportunity to engage with the province, but any process must begin with government-to-government dialogue in our traditional territories."[5]

He called the Far North Act a new form of colonialism.

Dayna Scott and John Cutfeet of the Yellowhead Institute, a First Nations–led research group, agreed.[6] "The FNA's fatal flaw is that it purports to give the government the ultimate and unilateral authority to approve mining developments, or roads and other infrastructure, even if those decisions run contrary to community land use plans," the pair said in a mid-2019 blog post.

The whole notion that impoverished northern communities had the resources to devise complex land use plans — determining which lands will be dedicated to protection and which will be open for potential economic development such as forestry, mining, and tourism — was equally flawed. It seemed another rigid requirement imposed upon them by settlers when in fact they have been doing their own type of planning for centuries.

"While sounding good in principle, it was an unfunded mandate thrust upon First Nations communities having no internal capacity or structure to organize and complete," Cliffs' Richard Fink commented later. "As usual with the province, they provide plenty of lip service and limited assistance. These plans became a quagmire."

The traditional territories outlined by the four communities that did devise land use plans — Attawapiskat, Eabametoong, Marten Falls, and Webequie — are all vast and overlap like a Venn diagram. That makes sense because they are based more on trap lines and shared river access than any formal jurisdictional boundary, but complicates negotiations about who gets what in relation to resource development.[7]

The simplistic assumption that Indigenous people are universally anti-development has led to flawed policy-making not just in Ontario, but across Canada. In mid-2021, an Alberta judge rebuked the federal government for engaging in one-sided consultation favouring First Nations that oppose resource extraction over those that offer their support. In this case, the Ermineskin Cree in western Alberta won their case against Ottawa, which had ordered a full federal impact assessment on the Vista coal mine expansion without consulting them. The Ermineskin, who had negotiated Impact and Benefit Agreements with Coalspur Mines, argued that they had a right to an uninterrupted livelihood and that Indigenous peoples' economic realities must not be reduced to traditional activities only.

The next year, an Alberta court of appeal went a step further, declaring the federal environmental assessment in the Ring of Fire incompatible with Indigenous autonomy and unconstitutional, a "legislative creep" that interferes with the division of power between the federal and provincial governments guaranteed in the constitution.[8]

"[The Ermineskin] case makes explicit what many of us have observed over the years: Indigenous people who support resource development do not fall comfortably into mainstream Canada's idealized version of what Indigenous people should and shouldn't do, and they are therefore ignored," wrote Heather Exner-Pirot, a research advisor to the Indigenous Resource Network and a fellow at the Macdonald-Laurier Institute, in an opinion piece for the *National Post*.[9]

With the change in provincial leadership in 2018, it was Doug Ford's turn to take a crack at the North. His government vowed to dismantle the FNA in the interests of reducing "red tape" and "regulatory burdens" in Ontario. Instead, the provincial government tabled Bill 132, the Better for People, Smarter for Business Act, meant to pare down regulation in a wide range of areas, including the environment, agriculture, food safety, alcohol, mining, and insurance.

But NAN's Chief Fiddler knew what new laws cloaked in sunny verbiage would mean for *his* people. He said the bill "seriously undermines the mining industry's obligation to consult with First Nation communities,"[10] once again expressing his frustration with Ontario's leaders and lawmakers.

The province doubled down in its fall 2021 mini-budget by proposing more tinkering with the FNA to increase the potential for resource extraction in the North, including helping "significant legacy infrastructure projects," such as all-season roads for First Nation communities and the Ring of Fire. The amendments would remove both protection for 225,000 square kilometres of land and provisions prohibiting development in areas that did not have a community-based land use plan in place.

In a significant change of heart, NAN backed the new plan to facilitate economic development and enhance collaboration between the province and First Nations.

"Nishnawbe Aski Nation and the Ministry of Northern Development, Mines, Natural Resources and Forestry engaged in a joint process to review and recommend updates to the Far North Act," said Derek Fox, who was elected NAN grand chief in 2021 to replace Fiddler. "We are pleased to have had this opportunity to work together and that the outcomes of that process are reflected in the proposed amendments to the Act."[11]

But Neskantaga, a member of NAN, remained unconvinced anything had been resolved with respect to Indigenous consultation in the Ring of Fire. The tiny community of 300 fired back with a legal challenge over the Ontario government's plan to build the Northern Road Link through what it considers its "homelands." This time Neskantaga named neighbouring Marten Falls First Nation, a proponent of the Indigenous-led environmental assessment of the road, as a respondent in the suit.[12]

You could say that Doug Ford's divide and conquer approach had worked. But what did it achieve, other than further fracturing relationships among tiny and troubled First Nations communities?

CHAPTER 12

Planes, Trains, or Automobiles?

A high-pitched whine from the dashboard startles Alex Debogorski from his focus on the road ahead. His air pressure dial has hit the red zone. He stops and leaps out of his big rig, loaded with 22,000 pounds of diamond processing sand, into temperatures broaching minus-40 degrees Celsius. Diving under the truck, he twists his torso and sprawls on the ice to inspect the underbelly with a tiny flashlight.[1]

Sure enough, the dryer for the air brakes has failed and ice is building up in the system. He's leaking air. Without enough pressure, his brakes will lock and become useless. It's sundown in the Northwest Territories, somewhere between Debogorski's last rest stop north of Yellowknife and the Ekati diamond mine at the northern end of the 400-kilometre ice road. He's been driving for hours.

Debogorski is a veteran trucker on the winter roads of northern Canada and a celebrity thanks to *Ice Road Truckers*, a popular reality TV show that ran for eleven seasons on the History Channel. He knows risk. But his brow is furrowed. To avoid losing all his air, he'll have to stop every few kilometres to shimmy underneath the truck and reset the dryer. It's his only choice. That or remain idling on the lake, waiting for help, and risk crashing though the surface to a slushy grave — taking the show's director with him — as the weight and vibration of the truck buckle the ice and then crack it wide open.

It's going to be a long, ass-numbing night.

Ice buildup in the compressor that powers the air brakes is a common problem for truckers plying the roughly 10,000 kilometres of frozen winter roads in Canada. But it's just one of many risks they're willing to take to earn a year's salary, C$100,000 or more, during the two to three months the roads stay open: "dash for the cash," they call it.

You need the fearlessness of a gladiator to pursue a career in which your life depends on the ice holding while all around you it cracks like thunder and pops like a shotgun blast. You need the serenity of a yogi to travel at a 20-kilometre-per-hour crawl to prevent your truck's forward momentum from forming waves under the ice that could explode upward as you inch closer to shore.

Most ice road truckers don't have enough of either trait to make it through a season. They lose their nerve. Some have to be airlifted out after delivering their first load because they are afraid to make the return trip. The ones who persevere walk the line between bravado and caution.

"The first couple of times, it's extremely scary," the veteran Debogorski, a devout Christian and father of eleven, told the talk show *Profiles*. "But you generally lose more equipment than lives. We've probably lost, in northern Canada, something in the vicinity of about 50 men over 35 or 40 years, but we've probably lost triple that in equipment."

The first documented settler use of ice roads in Canada took place in January 1935.[2] A convoy of sixteen tractors pulling sleighs loaded with tonnes of mining equipment travelled 222 kilometres along a road cut through the bush to an unidentified mine in northern Canada. The first tractor took ten days to reach the mine site. Another three months passed before the job was complete. According to *Popular Mechanics*, one of the tractors, carrying four men, crashed through lake ice. The tractor was retrieved. There was no mention of what happened to the men.

Then, in the 1940s, Svein Sigfusson, the enterprising son of Icelandic immigrants in Manitoba, saw the potential of using frozen lakes and rivers to transport the bounty of fish caught in Canada's northern lakes to markets in Winnipeg and Chicago. He started to use tractors to pull sleighs laden with pickerel and whitefish across miles of wilderness.[3] He went on to form a successful business building ice roads and transporting goods to and from remote communities previously cut off from the world.

But until the demands of World War II forced manufacturers to design more reliable trucks, only tracked vehicles such as snowmobiles and Caterpillars could ply the limited ice roads. It was a slow and dismal business.

Frustrated by the time it took for the "cat trains" to reach mine sites he supplied in the Northwest Territories, John Denison, a former RCMP officer, started engineering roads that could handle the new and improved wheeled trucks. Soon, thousands of kilometres of winter roads were being built, including the road that would eventually service the diamond mines Alex Debogorski drove on half a century later. In 1998 Denison received the Order of Canada for opening up the North to development.

Denison's road-building technique has since been perfected and now, for the most part, First Nations communities build and maintain Canada's ice roads. Counterintuitive as it may seem, the routes are designed to cross as many lakes as possible because it's much easier to build and drive on a road when there is no bush to contend with and surfaces are flat. On land sections, the operators have to cut down trees and pack down snow to smooth and level the surface.

Before any road building can take place, surveyors use ground-penetrating radar tethered to snowmobiles or amphibious vehicles to measure the thickness of the ice and ensure it can withstand thousands of pounds of truck and cargo. The radar antenna sends 400-MHz radio waves down into the lake. A computer calculates the ice thickness based on the time it takes the signal to return from the ice-water contact. Once the thickness reaches the height of an average five-year-old, it's safe for a super B tanker fully loaded with 48,000–50,000 litres of fuel to proceed.[4]

Next, snowplows push the snow aside to make sure the road surface benefits from exposure to freezing air temperatures rather than being insulated by snow cover. The plow drivers take the biggest risks because although their vehicles aren't as heavy, the ice is still forming as they work. Later, drillers confirm the ice thickness indicated by the radar measurements and pump water from the lake to flood the roadway to make it more stable. Finally, a notched plow blade scores the surface to provide a modicum of traction.

The ice road serving the Ekati ("fat lake" in Tlicho), Gahcho Kué ("big rabbit lake" in Chipewyan), and Diavik diamond mines (where

Debogorski's air compressor broke down) is known as the Tibbitt to Contwoyto Winter Road. Denison himself built a leg of the road in the 1960s. It was reconstructed in 1982 to supply the since closed Lupin gold mine, 568 kilometres north of Tibbitt Lake, the point where the road begins just east of Yellowknife. The road was revived again in the 1990s when Ekati went into production — Canada's first diamond mine and the discovery that touched off diamond exploration across the country, inadvertently leading to Neil Novak's base metal discovery in the Ring of Fire.

In 2019, the twentieth anniversary of the section of the route that leads to the diamond mines, it took 400 workers and C$20 million to prepare the road for a February 1 opening. That season, about 800 drivers in more than 8,300 trucks departed from Yellowknife to make the trip to the mines.[5] To mark the anniversary, the three mine operators dispensed C$5,000 cash prizes to their most valued drivers, on top of the routine cash awards given to the safest drivers each year.

In return, the mine operators extracted roughly C$2 billion worth of diamonds that year alone and saved millions of dollars in transportation costs they would otherwise have incurred by flying in equipment and supplies. Without the ice roads, it's unlikely they would generate enough profits to operate.

But are the ice roads also the problem? As its name suggests, the Tibbitt to Contwoyto Winter Road once stretched much further north, all the way to Contwoyto Lake. There, on the north shore of the lake, stood the tiny, ambitious Jericho diamond mine, which remarkably had secured a marketing agreement with Tiffany & Co., the renowned New York jewellery dealer. It seemed like a guaranteed cash cow.

But a particularly warm season in 2006, Jericho's first year of production, set off a chain of events that shattered that notion. That year, the road lasted only 40 days instead of the customary 60 to 70 days before melting too much to be safe. Tahera Diamond Corporation — the now-defunct company that operated the mine — had to revise its original mining plan to compensate for the resulting lack of supplies.[6] To conserve fuel, the company mined the more accessible but less valuable ore at surface instead of digging down to get at the high grade. Equipment breakdowns that would normally be just an inconvenience, coupled with a low Canadian dollar, put the already stretched company over the edge. In 2007, the diamond grades (hence profit margins) were just not good enough to save the troubled mine. Tahera declared bankruptcy in 2008. Its leg of the road was abandoned to the ever-warming elements.

Between 1948 and 2016, the annual mean temperature in Canada's north increased by 2.3 degrees Celsius, about three times the global rate.[7] The warming is projected to accelerate. Along the Hudson and James Bay coastlines, near where the Ring of Fire is located, average winter temperatures could rise by a further 5 degrees by 2050. What happened at Jericho is sure to repeat itself in the rest of Canada's Far North.

At most significant risk are the First Nations, Métis, and Inuit communities that rely on the ice roads to supply life-sustaining necessities including fuel, medical equipment, and building materials. The price tag to fly in these supplies would be exorbitant for communities already struggling with poverty and housing shortages.

As a result, many Indigenous people desire all-season roads to their communities. Reflecting on the Inuvik–Tuktoyaktuk (or Inuvik–Tuk) highway that opened in the Arctic in 2017, Crystal Gail Fraser, a Gwichyà Gwich'in woman, wrote:

> The colonial perspective (as roads as a nation building or resource extraction exercise) makes it easy to overlook the role of Tuktuyaaqtuuq residents, local business owners, and Dinjii Zhuh and Inuvialuit politicians and lobbyists who advocated for the highway — and what it should look like and who should build it — over the past several decades. For them, the road was not about celebrating a colonial vision. An all-weather highway had practical, immediate benefits: local Indigenous-owned businesses won the contract to build the highway, and its construction would not only help reduce food insecurity but also inject much-needed work into local economies, including tourism.[8]

Winter roads are becoming unsustainable anyway. The glory days, when Denison and Sigfusson opened up the North by building roads that were there one day and gone the next, are over. That's part of the reason Kathleen Wynne's government pledged in 2014 to invest a billion dollars to build a permanent all-weather road into the Ring of Fire and its surrounding communities, instead of simply extending an existing network of winter roads.

"I knew I wouldn't consider my mandate to be successful if we didn't get shovels in the ground," Wynne said to me after her term as premier was over.

✳

Ontario's corridors of power are strangely empty for a Monday in March. I can hear my footsteps echoing on the tile floor and I don't encounter a single soul as I make my way to Wynne's office, tucked away in a wing of the legislative building at Queen's Park. The House is not sitting that day, so the security screening apparatus that leads to the public gallery is cordoned off with red ribbon.

It's an extraordinarily warm day for the season, light jacket weather, but I can imagine shivering on a more typical winter day in this cavernous wing, rebuilt after a 1909 fire with cold white marble and tile. Most of the heavy wooden doors embedded with frosted glass are closed, including that of Wynne's former minister of Northern Development and Mines Michael Gravelle, but Wynne's is propped wide open. Her elderly assistant greets me warmly in her anteroom, and Wynne herself emerges moments later, dressed in a dusty-rose blazer that matches the spring-like day. She shakes my hand enthusiastically, ushers me in, and shuts the heavy door behind her, eager to get on with a packed day for the former premier turned Liberal MPP.

Her airy, sun-filled office facing south over Lake Ontario looks like a home away from home. To the left of her desk, there's a gallery of photos of Wynne attending various public events, but my eye is drawn front and centre to a photo of Wynne and her partner planting a kiss on each cheek of their beaming daughter, bedecked in graduation regalia. Two armchairs are lined up in front of the window, at a right angle to a couch. I seat myself in one of them. After double-checking a few agenda details with her assistant, Wynne settles in the middle of the couch.

Her crushing loss to Conservative Doug Ford in 2018 is behind her. The tears of her concession speech are dry, and somehow, though Wynne stepped down as party leader, she survived as a representative and kept her Don Valley West seat, one of just eight Liberal seats left in the 124-seat Ontario legislature.

I'm not sure if she's reviewed any notes before our meeting, but her recall on the Ring of Fire is impressive; perhaps unsurprising given that she spent two years of her tenure actively trying to hammer home a deal with the nine First Nations — the Matawa Tribal Council — whose traditional territory includes the Ring of Fire. She says it irks her that Premier Ford appears to be using all the efforts she and her colleagues made to pave a path of reconciliation to ram through roads without further consultation. Just a few days before our meeting, Ford announced a deal with two of the nine First Nations, Webequie and Marten Falls, to get the north-south road built.

"A government like this one pretends that they can just come in and, because of who they are and their bully tactics, get a deal when we couldn't — that gives the public the idea that somehow all you need to do is be forceful. That's just not true," she says, her piercing blue eyes locked onto mine. "We're in a very delicate era when it comes to Indigenous and non-Indigenous relationships. I can easily see blockades on those road construction projects in the North."

Wynne interrupts herself to request a two-minute break and heads for the door. It's the first day on the job for new provincial Liberal leader Steven Del Duca, who was transportation and economic development minister during her tenure as premier, and she wants to be on deck to welcome him back to the fold. The contempt she expressed for the current provincial leadership lingers in the air.

✳

Ontario has a network of about 3,000 kilometres of winter roads. Every year the provincial government budgets millions of dollars to build and maintain them (compared to billions spent on provincial highway infrastructure). In 2019, this road-building exercise amounted to almost C$6 million for roads to reach thirty-one First Nations in the Far North and the town of Moosonee on the southern tip of James Bay.

However, Quebec is years ahead of its neighbouring province in establishing a permanent road network to access resources and service communities in the North. So are other provinces, such as Alberta and B.C. Some have speculated that the reason Ontario is so far behind is because, as the traditional centre of commerce and manufacturing in Canada, Ontario's leaders never had to pursue their own natural resources. The resources came to them.

In 2015, Quebec launched Plan Nord, a road map to open up even more development in the province's North. By 2035, the Quebec government anticipates a total of C$50 billion in private and public investments, including C$2 billion on new roads, airports, and other public infrastructure. The investments would cover an enormous land mass, about 72 percent of the province, or 1.2 million square kilometres. Among other goals, the plan is expected to open up new opportunities for exploration and mining in the sparsely populated region, where a smattering of 120,000 souls, a third of them Indigenous, reside.

Plan Nord allowed Stornoway Diamonds, for example, to access a provincial loan to complete the 240-kilometre extension of Route 167 from Chibougamau to Renard, Quebec's first diamond mine, in north-central Quebec. Instead of flying in equipment, fuel, and crews by floatplane or helicopter, the operators were able to use the all-season road at considerably less cost. And in 2019, Quebec announced a C$1.75 million investment to connect Newmont's Éléonore gold mine, even further north in the James Bay watershed, to the existing regional fibre-optic network.

The Ring of Fire presents an opportunity to jumpstart similar access to Ontario's highways, fibre optics, and power lines for communities in the North. In 2022, the nearest all-season roads to the Ring of Fire were the seventy-year-old Highway 599, 300 kilometres to the southwest at Pickle Lake (a gold mining community near the Ojibway Mishkeegogamang Nation, and the most northerly town in Ontario to have a permanent road linking to the provincial highway system); and Highway 584, 340 kilometres to the south at Nakina. The nearest railways are similarly distant: the CN line at Sioux Lookout to the southwest, and the Algoma Central and Ontario Northland lines to the south at Hearst. There has been enough talk about potential transportation corridors to the Ring of Fire to fill a wing of Queen's Park with meeting minutes, and enough money spent to build considerable capacity within the affected communities. But very little action.

※

In early 2021, almost a year after Ontario inked a historic deal with Webequie and Marten Falls to build the Northern Road Link, the all-season road to their communities near the Ring of Fire, something unexpected happened. Frank Smeenk hired a former railway executive to fulfill his long-term dream to build rail to the region.

The rationale behind hiring veteran railroader Tony Marquis was that it would make more sense to move chromite ore, a bulk commodity similar to iron ore, by rail than by road. The proposed "tramway system" would be designed to annually transport 10 million tonnes of chromite over a 340-kilometre line between the town of Nakina and the Ring of Fire.

The ambitious undertaking would cost as much as C$2 billion and possibly form the catalyst for a network of rail infrastructure in the region. The plan included construction of a utility corridor along the route that would have branch connections to the First Nations in the region, eliminating the need for diesel power generation and providing optical fibre networks to the remote communities.

It was a new chapter in an old story. As explained previously, a decade earlier Smeenk's KWG Resources had achieved something equally unconventional: staked all the claims along an esker — a ridge of sand and gravel left over by a glacier as it retreats — running from the CP Rail line near Nakina north through the traditional territory of Marten Falls First Nation to the Ring of Fire. It was the only ground high and dry enough in the James Bay Lowlands to support a railway.

"Some people say this is proof that God is a mining engineer because he put a chromite deposit up there, and then he laid out a road for us," said KWG's vice-president of exploration and development, M.J. "Moe" Lavigne.[9]

Normally mining companies stake claims so they can explore for minerals. But in this case, Smeenk wanted to secure the ground so trains could move along it one day, helping to transport all manner of valuable metals from the Ring of Fire to processing plants and markets in the south and beyond.

KWG went a step further, hiring contractors to complete soil sampling along the esker to more accurately determine the ground conditions. When the contractors reached the Albany River near Marten Falls First Nation, they felled a pine tree on the banks of the river that marked the burial site of the late Chief Elias Moonias's ancestor. Though KWG issued an apology, the damage had been done. "An apology is not going to change the fact that they broke the law," Moonias said.[10]

So it came as a surprise to regional players when, in 2013, Ontario Mining Commissioner Linda Kamerman ruled in favour of KWG's right to control the land corridor. At the same time Kamerman denied a request for an easement by the American company Cliffs, which wished to build a road on the esker instead. The American company had outlined a "base-case" scenario to construct a C$600 million all-season road, running 340 kilometres north-south, with help from Ontario taxpayers.

The Cliffs proposal was unpopular because it implied that the road would be private and omit branch roads to nearby First Nations communities. Furthermore, based on Cliffs' projections that it would transport about 2.3 million tonnes of chromite out of the area per year, roughly 140 trips by trucks carrying 46 tonnes each would be needed every day. That's a lot of dust, fumes, and noise barrelling through a pristine boreal forest. Not to mention the potential for unrelenting roadkill.

Forging ahead, KWG hired engineering consulting firm Tetra Tech to run a cost analysis comparing the road and rail options. Because the chromite deposits were expected to remain in production for several years and maybe even decades, the consultants concluded it would be more economic over time to ship the ore by rail. Trains would also be more environmentally friendly than hundreds of diesel trucks making the daily journey. The "rail option is more robust, low maintenance, cost-reflective and demand-responsive to operational and market conditions than the road option," Tetra Tech wrote.[11]

But KWG's ability to throw its weight around in the region was fading as financing and other deals fell through. All over Canada, the railway dream was dying too. In 2012, unionized employees of Ontario Northern Transport Company attempted to buy their employer and build a publicly owned railway corridor to connect the Ring of Fire to existing rail lines, but failed for lack of government support. CN similarly cancelled a C$5 billion plan to build an 800-kilometre railway and terminal project to access iron ore mines being developed in Labrador, citing difficult logistics and markets. Low commodity prices contributed to the general reluctance to run expensive tracks into mineral-rich but remote areas.

Roads, on the other hand, despite being almost equally challenging to build in the unforgiving muskeg, were getting the go-ahead for construction, most notably on the Quebec side of James Bay. In Ontario, Wynne's 2014 pledge to help build a road to the Ring of Fire, and encourage the federal government to chip in, served as an enticing catalyst. A group called the East-West Ring of Fire Road Coalition favoured an east-west route. They lobbied for a road extending from Highway 599 at Pickle Lake to the Ring of Fire mineral belt. The group insisted the east-west route would serve a greater number of communities than a north-south route, align better with existing power lines, and bring more economic spinoffs from mining.

Noront and the provincial government preferred a north-south road, likely partly because they had already spent years negotiating with the communities along the proposed route and did not want to start from scratch with the communities to the west. Nickel and copper concentrates from the first mine, Eagle's Nest, would be bagged and loaded onto trucks at the mine site, then trucked to a rail-siding near Aroland First Nation, a Noront shareholder, for rail shipping to a smelter in northern Ontario.

As the road discussion progressed, Smeenk held fast to his rail vision. In 2016 he asked China Railway Construction, one of China's three major state-owned rail groups, to study design and financing options for building the railroad to the chromite deposits. The study estimated that the railroad could transport 10 million tonnes of chromite annually by 2030, potentially growing to a yearly volume of 24 million tonnes by 2040. In April that year, a delegation of Chinese engineers visited Parliament Hill along with Smeenk to promote the project to MP Marc Serré, the chair of Justin Trudeau's northern Ontario caucus. The following month, Marten Falls' Bruce Achneepineskum — who became chief after Elias Moonias's untimely death — flew to China to hear more about the plan to build a rail line through his community's traditional territory.

But nothing ever came of the negotiations. The Chinese engineers flew over the area in a helicopter, concluded there were no major construction barriers, entertained the KWG delegation in China, and were never heard from publicly again. Achneepineskum turned his attention and Marten Falls' limited resources to roads instead.

The nature of the landscape and the many river crossings will make building the road complicated. "When you fly over, it's like Queen Anne's lace," Wynne recalled. "There's more water than land. It became clear to me that we weren't building a road, we were building a causeway." And the cost escalated after Wynne's tenure to as much as C$1.6 billion in 2022, including funding for road planning and construction, environmental assessments, support for participants, and well-being initiatives in nearby First Nations. The province has asked the federal government to contribute about half this sum.

On March 2, 2020, Doug Ford presided over the press conference at the Prospectors & Developers Association of Canada convention in Toronto, announcing that the 120-kilometre Northern Road Link would become a reality. Webequie and Marten Falls would co-lead the environmental assessment of the two-lane all-weather road. The Northern Road Link would connect with two other proposed roads — the 200-kilometre Marten Falls-to-Aroland Community Access Road at the south end, and the proposed 110-kilometre Webequie Supply Road to the Ring of Fire at the north end — for a total of about 450 kilometres of new road.

"We are moving ahead with this agreement so all communities in the region can connect to the next phase, which is to secure and bring good-paying jobs in mining, construction, and other skilled trades to our communities," Marten Falls Chief Bruce Achneepineskum told the press conference's packed audience.

Two years later, he reiterated his support for the project in a press release announcing the next step, the terms of reference — or work plan — for the road's environmental assessment:

> Our partnership sets a new precedence in the region on Indigenous proponency. As we prepare to submit the Terms of Reference for the Northern Road Link project, it is important to remember why we are here and what this represents. We

are leading the Northern Road Link because the project is in our traditional territory and we are exercising our right to self-determination. This represents a potentially bright future for our future generations, for our neighbours, and for the region.

By this time, the road link to critical minerals in the North had become part of Ford's much grander plan to entice southern Ontario automakers to produce electric vehicles that rely on some of these minerals. "We're going to be the number one manufacturer of electric battery operated cars in North America. We're not only going to manufacture the batteries here, but also manufacture the cars,"[12] said Ford, who was reelected premier in 2022 and promptly appointed a new minister of mines with a mandate to develop the Ring of Fire.

But missing from the hype was a budget, a timeline, or any mention of further consultations with other First Nations communities along the proposed route. Complicating matters even further, the provincial road-building plan was running up against the federal government order to conduct a more holistic regional assessment of development in the Ring of Fire, under the terms of the new federal Impact Assessment Act. The project-by-project approval process for the roads flew in the face of the goals of regional assessment, as the Wildlands League made clear in its 2021 response to the Webequie Supply Road proposal:[13] "The single biggest concern with this proposed project assessment, from a comprehensive environmental assessment perspective, is that this subject project is being treated as a remote, unconnected road proposal, servicing a known temporary opportunity. And yet it cannot even be described without alluding to a host of additionally possible, and desired, development scenarios."

And what of the objections of the Mushkegowuk Council, representing some of the communities along the James Bay coast and downstream of the Ring of Fire? The railway to Moosonee that serves as such an important hub for these otherwise isolated communities was once a contender for ferrying the chromium and other metals from the Ring of Fire. Under one proposed plan, the railway would have been extended north from Moosonee to Attawapiskat and then west to the Ring of Fire.

The proposed corridor would house fibre-optic cables and a high-voltage energy transmission line.

Some of the infrastructure had already been completed. Five Nations Energy Inc. (FNEI), an Indigenous-owned energy transmission utility, built a 270-kilometre transmission line north along the James Bay shoreline from Moosonee two decades ago. The line follows the winter road through the communities of Fort Albany, Kashechewan, and Attawapiskat, replacing noisy, polluting diesel generators that relied on fuel transported by barge and winter road. When De Beers opened the Victor diamond mine on the Attawapiskat River in 2008, FNEI delivered electricity to the line connecting the mine and incorporated De Beers fibre-optic cables to bring internet access to the communities.

But the plan to build a railway to the Ring of Fire from Moosonee was ditched in favour of the north-south road from Nakina. Politics between the provincial government and First Nations groups may have played a part. The proposed road falls within the provincial riding of Kiiwetinoong, which covers the communities most likely to be directly affected, for better or worse, by the Ring of Fire development. Mushkegowuk–James Bay, encompassing Moosonee and the other communities along the James Bay coast, became a separate provincial riding in 2018 and potentially less influential in the Ring of Fire decision-making.

Intentional? Perhaps. But to appease the James Bay coastal communities, the province promised to "explore" the idea of a permanent all-season road linking the communities on the James Bay coast to the provincial road network after some of the Mushkegowuk Council communities strongly opposed the Ring of Fire development.

KWG's latest attempt to build the railway to the Ring of Fire, under newly elected president Megan McElwain, seems equally fraught with complications. But railroader Tony Marquis is excited about his new role as head of Canada Chrome Corporation, a wholly owned subsidiary of KWG established to develop the rail plan. He believes road and rail connections to the James Bay Lowlands do not have to be mutually exclusive and that there will be a resurgence of rail worldwide as nations attempt to green their economies.

"I'm doing this because I'm intrigued by it and it's great for the North," Marquis told the *Sudbury Star*.[14] "It's great to open up prosperity for the

First Nations and [the Ring of Fire's] been wallowing for 12 years now, so I think it's time to do a reboot and get moving with it."

CONCLUSION

Keep the Faith

It's July 2020. We're inching towards James Bay, praying for a prevailing southwesterly. The inland sea lies 100 kilometres downstream, descending like a skinny leg from the bulge of Hudson Bay. We can smell the salt in the air. But our forearms ache with her resistance to our arrival.

Fighting the headwinds and horizontal rain rolling in from the bay's western flank has become an almost daily struggle, hindering our progress along what we'd hoped would be an easy paddle harmonious with the current. As the sucker steering the yellow, 16-foot Prospector canoe, I've rarely felt more powerless than when the wind bats the stern around like a cat toying with a mouse. Our heads are mostly cast down to keep our eyes from tearing up, but we catch glimpses of bald eagles soaring overhead, hunting for prey. They're lording over the river, revelling in the very gusts we curse. Sometimes they perch high on the straggly branches of black spruce to peer down on us, this sideshow of human frailty.

For such a wild place, the rivers of the James Bay Lowlands are surprisingly orderly and evenly spaced.[1] Charging in from the south before emptying into the Moose River and draining into the open waters of James Bay at Moosonee, Ontario's only saltwater port, is the Missinaibi River. In the eighteenth century, the Missinaibi was the main fur-trading route between James Bay and Lake Superior, the largest of the Great Lakes. Stretching for 500 kilometres, it's one of the longest free-flowing protected river corridors in North America.

About 200 kilometres north of the Missinaibi lies the mighty Albany River, the longest river in Ontario. The Albany runs almost a thousand kilometres from its source on the Canadian Shield through the community of Marten Falls, then spills out at the Cree Nation of Fort Albany on James Bay. And a couple of hundred kilometres north again lies the Attawapiskat River watershed, where the Ring of Fire's mineral explorers toil and Cree and Ojibway fish and hunt. This river connects the two Nations most vocally opposed to mineral development: Neskantaga in the west and Attawapiskat on James Bay to the east. Though mostly inaccessible to protesters from the south, it will likely become the epicentre of protest if road construction to the Ring of Fire begins.

All three watersheds are generally flat, poorly drained, and blanketed in muskeg.

✳

As the first wave of the COVID pandemic was subsiding in Canada, our group from the Greater Toronto Area touched down on Bell's Bay, a remote campsite on the Missinaibi. Each of us had different reasons for the trip but were united in the joy of being released from COVID lockdown to explore our own backyard wilderness.

Our mission was a ten-day, 245-kilometre canoe adventure. Our destination was the southern tip of James Bay, 850 kilometres north of Toronto. Peering through the window of our float plane, the swampy muskeg below, punctured by stunted spruce trees, looked desolate and inhospitable. But along the coast, black bears and caribou roam and migratory birds feed.

We felt extraordinarily lucky and joyful as the Turbo Beaver landed and glided towards the riverbank to drop the last of our crew and gear, then took back to the air, sun-dappled wings tipped in farewell. All there was left to do was load up the canoes and point them downstream. Easy, right?

Not so. The wind is like that friend who coaxes you along, pretending to be on your side, then stabs you in the back when you least expect it. We quickly developed a love-hate relationship with her. We'd rejoice when she had our back. We'd groan when she turned against us or mischievously made off with our featherlight tents.

And we'd mourn her loss when the bugs came to feast.

At the mere hint of a lull, an Air Force of black flies, mosquitoes, and horseflies filled the vacuum, crawling up our pant legs and noses and gathering mercilessly on the baby-soft underbelly of our chins where we hadn't thought to apply bug repellent. Even the women among us scratched our faces absentmindedly as if sporting a five-day growth.

What prompted this madness? I blame Kathleen Wynne. When I interviewed her for this book, she mentioned a canoe trip in the James Bay Lowlands she had taken with her partner; she had wanted to better understand the remote area as she tried to negotiate a regional framework with the Matawa Tribal Council to develop the Ring of Fire mineral deposits. She knew building mines in the area would be a challenge, partly because of the fragile ecosystem and partly because there were no roads, no railways, and no permanent energy source.

Wynne recalled flying into the region, seeing the expanse of bog and swamp below, and immediately recognizing how equally difficult it would be to establish transportation infrastructure there. Another factor that struck her, other than all that water, was the remoteness of the Indigenous communities. On a subsequent canoe trip on the Yukon River, she noticed that the communities there benefited from the connection of the river; they were gradually recovering their ownership of land and self-governance after the shock and disruption of the Klondike gold rush in the late nineteenth century and the residential school abuses of the twentieth. The James Bay Lowlands communities are much more isolated from one another. Of the nine First Nations communities that form the Matawa Tribal Council, only four are accessible by an all-weather road. The rest rely on air transport or winter roads offering shorter and shorter seasons as the climate warms.

As our float plane ferries us to the launch point, I try to imagine what flying over the Ring of Fire two decades from now might be like.

In my mind's eye, there is a thin strip of road winding its way north for more than 400 kilometres from a paved highway to a tiny cluster of dots representing the mines site's offices, accommodations, and processing plant. At about the halfway mark, the road branches off east to the community of Marten Falls at the confluence of the Albany and Ogoki Rivers and west to Neskantaga and Eabametoong.

Barely visible from the sky in 2020, Marten Falls has grown. Off-reserve band members have moved back and started families. Housing built to accommodate the expanding community and replace inadequate dwellings spreads out concentrically from the town centre. From the sky you can see the roof of the community centre that houses a hockey arena and an indoor soccer pitch. At the north end of the mine road, another branch heads west to Nibinamik and a larger centre at Webequie, also swelling with newcomers who have flocked there to join the new mining economy and be part of a thriving community.

But other than the community nodes and the mine site, the area remains the same wilderness that has existed there for millennia. Looking east along the Attawapiskat River, I can't even make out the outline of the pit where the Victor diamond mine once operated. It's long since been filled in. Nature has done the rest of the healing.

✳

"Which would you rather have, the cold and wind or the bugs?" I poll the group, retrieving another squished and bloody blackfly from the crease behind my ear. Everyone agrees they'd take inclement weather over bugs any day. We're feeling somewhat less euphoric than when we touched down at our starting point in Bell's Bay. It seems it's always one evil or the other.

Save for the thriving insect scene (by some estimates, the density of mosquitoes is more than twelve million per hectare),[2] the soaring eagles, the dive-bombing kingfishers, some skittish mergansers, and a couple of shiny otters sliding playfully down the grey clay embankments, the shores are mostly silent and devoid of life. Where are the moose and bear we were certain we'd see? Had they fallen victim to hunters, or quietly succumbed to the changing climate? Were they hiding deeper in the bush, feeling less dependent on the river in this relative bounty of summer?

I feel an eeriness to this wide, shallow, meandering river. The signature black spruce trees that dominate the shoreline are bone thin and stark as if courting death. We encounter empty patches of bush where a wildfire has torn through. But sometimes it's hard to tell the charred trees from the healthy ones. The sky is gargantuan and intimidating. We are tiny and vulnerable, enveloped in an unsettling silence.

So perhaps it's fitting that we don't see another human soul outside our own bubble of nine trippers on this forlorn river. And yet we are a little surprised. Other adventurers are missing out. Peel back the surface layer of desolation, and beneath lies a rich cultural history, unique geology, and a globally significant ecology. It's a privilege to find ourselves in one of the last pockets on Earth largely undisturbed by human influence.

Indeed, the far northern Ontario region that includes the rivers we are lucky to paddle "is one of the world's largest, most intact ecological systems, reflecting a high level of ecological integrity and providing ecosystem services far beyond its borders," according to Ontario's Far North Advisory Panel.[3]

There are hints of this richness everywhere: in the arc of a sturgeon's back as it leaps from the water; in the fossils left over from the ancient inland sea that litter the sand and gravel bars; in the golf-course green of the grasses swaying in the wind along the shoreline.

In a word, the James Bay Lowlands — as stark and unforgiving as they seem from a distance — are fragile. They deserve our care and attention.

*

As we paddle against the wind, my mind returns to an imagined future for the Ring of Fire. The same winds we curse are being harvested to power the mines using high-efficiency turbines. During the rare times the wind is not blowing, energy is stored in batteries manufactured using nickel mined onsite and processed in the south. A hydrogen plant complements the turbines, fuelling the haul and transport trucks and storing added energy to help power the mines. By switching to wind energy and hydrogen, the mine managers have weaned themselves off their traditional dependence on fossil fuels.

Drones fly overhead, carrying parts and supplies to and fro, identifying production bottlenecks, and monitoring for approaching wildlife or irregularities in the surrounding watershed. Indigenous businesses in Webequie and Marten Falls provide all of the mine services, from catering to autonomous trucking.

Underground, precision robots work the mine faces to extract valuable ore without disrupting any of the surrounding rock. Where the mineralization is more broadly disseminated, specially engineered organisms feed exclusively on it, separating out the valuable from the barren rock. In both cases, the techniques produce about 75 percent less waste than the typical twenty-first-century mine. Sensors throughout the mines identify trouble spots where rockfalls might occur and detect leaks in the water system or dips in air quality that could gum up the working robots. Human miners no longer venture underground themselves, except to troubleshoot. Instead, they operate safely from surface to control self-driving trucks and loaders used to transport the payload.

Any waste rock produced is stored underground in mined-out areas, essentially putting the rock back where it came from. Tailings from the processing plant are reintroduced as paste backfill (with the consistency of wet concrete) in smaller voids to avoid surface disposal and its inherent dangers. Every litre of water used in the mining and processing is recycled in a continuous closed loop, curtailing the amount of water required for extraction and preventing accidental leaks of contaminated water into the environment.

Under a unique 49 percent–51 percent joint venture between Wyloo and the Matawa Collective called ROF Mining, the underground base metals mines and surrounding communities are thriving. Wyloo provides the exploration and mining expertise and training. The Matawa Collective ensures the operations follow environmental and cultural regulations and protocols while managing its share of the mine revenue on behalf of First Nations affected by the Ring of Fire development.

By this point in 2040, the Eagle's Nest nickel-copper-platinum group metals deposit, the first of the Ring of Fire deposits to be mined, is getting long in the tooth. A surety bond has been set aside to finance reclamation, including re-establishing the bog and fen wetland over a square kilometre of disturbed surface above the mine workings. ROF has moved on to concurrently mine Blackbird, the first of four chromite mines. Blackbird shares the same underground infrastructure as Eagle's Nest, so the disturbance at surface has been minimal. Once the ore runs out at Blackbird, ROF will close it and move to the next underground mine that can provide maximum output with minimum disturbance: either one of the other chromite deposits or one of the several deposits of copper-zinc or nickel discovered through exploration.

ROF Mining has been granted a certificate that allows the joint venture to charge a premium for the metals produced. The certificate system has been designed as a globally sanctioned effort to weed out exploitative or dirty miners and reward socially and environmentally responsible ones. By upholding the highest standards of practice, the Ring of Fire mines have become a supplier of choice for manufacturers not just in Canada but worldwide. Using blockchain technology, stakeholders can trace all the materials from the mines, from the moment of extraction to shipment and finally to point of sale and use, ensuring best practices and transparency throughout the life cycle of the minerals. Valuable ore blocks are measured in kilograms, rather than the traditional tonnes, and the market for them is established well before extraction takes place. The joint venture shares the resultant tracking information and performance data with nearby communities in real time so that residents can see if, say, there has been an incremental drop in air quality, or an ore block has gone missing somewhere along the supply chain.

Discoveries made in the region since the first hit in 2007 mean there is enough carefully managed mineral supply to last for centuries, fuelling Canada's electric vehicle and green technology manufacturing sector. And under a unique partnership with the province, the joint venture has built a massive geological database that helps the region's Indigenous geoscientists find more orebodies and achieve a better understanding of their formation and distribution.

✳

If I'd had more time and whitewater paddling experience, the geoscientist in me would have opted for a longer canoe trip, beginning at the river's source in Missinaibi Lake where the Canadian Shield of hard pink granites and gneisses dominate and the rapids run fierce. That route runs through an important continental contact zone at Thunderhouse Falls, where the Canadian Shield abruptly meets the softer limestones of the lowlands. As the Missinaibi spills over Thunderhouse Falls, the river enters the northern range of the largest block of undisturbed boreal forest in the world. The river slows and widens, leaving its powerful, roaring energy behind on the Shield. The surrounding landscape is as flat as a prairie field, except where old shorelines left behind from the Tyrrell Sea's retreat form thin, low parallel ridges up to 100 kilometres inland.[4] Experiencing the geological transition would have been thrilling. Instead I chose just the last part of the route, relishing the delusion of floating down a lazy river to the bay.

As we paddle downstream, boulders the size of small cars jut out from the river like the monumental statues of Easter Island. They bore witness to the power of the Laurentide Ice Sheet that once blanketed the land. As it heaved and sighed with shifting temperatures, the glacier gouged giant fragments from the bedrock, carried them great distances, and dumped them wherever it wanted. Aside from a natural history lesson, the boulders served as early warning signals of shoals ahead threatening to ground our canoe before my bowman could bellow "Rocks ahead!" over the din of wind and rain.

The rivers in this part of the world are shallow at the best of times. At least one trip group we knew of had to drag their canoe for eight kilometres before the water levels could support their weight again. We were luckier, only grounding on shoals a couple of times a day. It became a point of pride among our group to figure out how to avoid these hidden traps by reading the hues and eddies of the water, listening to the language of the river and the wisdom of our guides.

Lining the riverbanks are poorly drained soils. They can support a diversity of trees such as spruce, balsam fir, trembling aspen, and white birch, but we mostly encounter emerald-green meadow marshes backed by black spruce as we approach James Bay. Behind that monotonous shoreline facade lurks an impenetrable jungle of alders that eventually bleeds into bog. Our guides demonstrate great psychological and physical fortitude by plunging into this bug-infested jungle to search for firewood every evening, the alders pushing back against them as they reach for that perfect log or simply one that would burn. Each time they emerge smiling and victorious, fresh-bleeding scratches on their faces and hands, like the Amazons of mythology, only much kinder.

The equally kinder, gentler gravel bars in the middle of the river harbour a plethora of plants and grasses. Some are extraordinary, like the yellow wildflowers connected by a network of red roots that creep along the surface of the glacial debris, seeking water and nutrients in lieu of moist soil. Their scientific name is *Potentilla anserina* L., also known as silverweed, used by humans for millennia to ward off evil spirits and as a food crop resembling parsnips.[5]

Beauty mixed with rarity and intrigue — a lowlands specialty.

✳

As we approach the communities at the mouth of the Moose River, my mind wanders again to an optimistic vision of what the communities near the Ring of Fire might become, assuming mine development proceeds. In my vision, the federal government has scrapped the Indian Act and stopped clawing back resource revenue from First Nations. The majority of government funds required to administer the Indian Act has been redirected towards delivering much-needed capacity to northern communities.

The First Nations of Ontario's James Bay Lowlands have seized the opportunity to become self-governing and self-sufficient. They have used the Agreement on Cree Nation Governance on the Quebec side of the bay as a model. Under that agreement, the Quebec Cree have the power to write their own laws on a variety of local governance issues affecting their communities, including environmental protection, public order, and land and resource use and planning.

Marten Falls, by virtue of being the halfway point between the provincial road network and the mine site, has become a hub for education and small business. Acrid wafts of burned diesel no longer permeate the air because diesel generators have been replaced by wind turbines supplemented by hydro power humming its way along transmission lines parallel to the north-south gravel road. Entrepreneurs using seed capital supplied by ROF Mining have spawned a network of businesses specializing in outdoor recreation and wilderness travel, cold weather clothing and equipment, mine service and supply, and traditional cooking.

The Matawa Collective has established a fund to reinvest the money flowing from its 51 percent share of revenue from Ring of Fire mines back into all of the region's communities. The revenue has financed the construction of elementary schools and hospitals, community centres, and other public infrastructure. Sustainable housing suited to the harsh but warming northern climate has replaced mouldy, drafty, sinking structures. The new houses are connected to sewers, electricity, and broadband providing high-speed internet access. Locally trained technicians manage and monitor the water treatment plants to ensure clean drinking water.

Indigenous teachers staff the community elementary schools and Indigenous doctors and nurses the hospitals. Mine employees enjoy flexibility in their work schedules so that they can venture out on the land in the spring and fall to participate in traditional hunting and harvesting practices and lay food in for the winter. Sponsored cultural events within the communities have returned some of the Indigenous language and identity lost during Canada's brutal attempts at assimilation.

More broadly, the Ontario government is redirecting tax revenues generated by the Ring of Fire into a Sovereign Wealth Fund for all Ontarians. The fund is designed to get northern citizens off the roller-coaster ride of commodity boom-bust cycles and ensure future generations benefit from the extraction of non-renewable resources. In this, Ontario has followed Norway, which started putting the revenue generated from offshore oil and gas production into a savings fund called the Government Pension Fund in 1996. By 2040 the value of Norway's fund had hit US$3 trillion.

Meanwhile, the Canadian government has helped retool the nation's car manufacturing plants to create an international hub for electric vehicle and EV battery production. As part of the plan, the government has mandated that materials required for the vehicles and batteries, such as nickel, be sourced only from mines meeting the highest global environmental standards — in other words, mines emulating those in the Ring of Fire.

✳

On day eight of the trip, we reach the mouth of the Moose River. The two communities located there are Moosonee and Moose Factory, whose combined population is about 4,000. The island community of Moose Factory, part of the reserve lands of the Moose Cree First Nation, was the first English-speaking settlement in Ontario and the second Hudson's Bay

Company post in North America. Hence the name "factory," as in factor, meaning the business agent for a trading company.

Across the river on the mainland lies Moosonee. The town was originally settled in 1903 by the Réveillon Frères of Paris as a fur-trading post to compete with Moose Factory. In 1932, the province extended a railway line to Moosonee from the south, making the town an important transportation hub for the Far North. Residents frequently travel between the two sister communities, by boat in the summer, ice road in the winter, and helicopter during the spring and fall, when the ice is breaking up or freezing.

We've had to adjust our itinerary to avoid Moose Factory, where COVID restrictions remain in place to protect vulnerable First Nations communities. We camp on an island in nearby Tidewater Provincial Park instead. The rest site sounds majestic but I find it spooky: it's littered with garbage and overrun by giant hogweed, an invasive garden plant from Asia that leaves severe burns on human skin. We hear a woman screaming in the night, from whence we cannot tell.

Sore, sleep-deprived, and swollen with bug bites — in a word, bushed — I'm eager to get back to the comforts of the city. Instead, the next morning we hitch a ride on a motorboat out to the open water of James Bay with Anne — a Cree woman from Moose Factory who survived the Sixties Scoop, another Canadian government assimilation program that took Indigenous kids from their own families and communities and placed them with white families mostly in the south. She's found her way back home. As she tells tales of trauma, we breathe in the salty air, then stop on an island that belongs to the territory of Nunavut, as all the islands in James Bay do.

We pack up our tents one last time and rally ourselves for a final paddle across the river to Moosonee, where we'll board the Polar Bear Express train heading south. There, I get my own taste of the ramifications of drinking tainted water, filling my bottle at a tap and later coming down with a bad case of giardiasis, an intestinal infection caused by the giardia parasite.

We're at the end of our journey, having just paddled though one of the most pristine wildernesses in the world. But the Ring of Fire discovery has complicated the region's future. Should the area remain relatively untouched, a crucible of biodiversity left to play its part in stemming climate change and providing a refuge for increasingly threatened wildlife? Or should it become a source of economic prosperity for the impoverished communities in the region? Is sustainable development an oxymoron in this fragile land?

I'll wager it isn't. I'm optimistic that the First Nations in the region will be able to negotiate a better life, just like their brethren on the Quebec side of James Bay did half a century ago. And I believe the key to that future is the Ring of Fire. The pieces are falling into place for this remarkable metal endowment to become a global model of sustainable resource development: another Sudbury, but with a much more balanced and equitable approach to First Nations and the environment, and a chance for the lowland communities to become self-governing directors of their own economic and social fate.

The backbone of my opinion is informed by the hard-fought legal battles won by First Nations over the past couple of decades. It is no small deal that they have insisted on, and secured, the right to be consulted and accommodated when development takes place on their traditional territories. Recognition and enforcement of that fundamental right has changed everything. Throughout its history, Canada's vast resources have been plundered by settlers. Indigenous residents were denied a share of the resulting riches, even left to suffer the poisonous environmental legacy in some cases. Now they have the leverage and public support to negotiate jobs, training, and equity interests in resource projects across the country while honouring a sense of duty to protect the land for generations to come.

The world is also awakening to the importance of preserving peatlands as carbon stores in the fight against climate change. And of protecting biodiversity. The Ring of Fire represents just 1.6 percent of the Hudson and James Bay lowlands land mass, but the roads and other infrastructure required to operate the mines must be constructed and managed to mitigate environment impacts on the peatlands. The federal government's comprehensive regional assessment of the sensitive area, in true partnership with Indigenous communities, is key to flagging potential hazards before it's too late to stop them. This is the first complete assessment under Canada's new Impact Assessment Act, so there is a lot at stake. It's worth taking the time to get it right and set a precedent for resource projects going forward.

The Ontario government needs more patience too. Driving a wedge between the communities near the Ring of Fire by building all-weather roads to communities that support infrastructure and mining development, while leaving others to flounder, practically guarantees that the Ring of Fire will be bogged down in legal wrangling over who has the right to what land for another dozen years. This would heap tragedy upon tragedy and be a blow to reconciliation.

With demand for nickel, copper, and the other metals in the Ring of Fire forecast to grow rapidly in the next few decades as the world moves away from fossil fuels and electrifies energy and transport, the region stands to be a long-lasting sustainable source of raw materials needed to build this green, low-carbon economy. There is no reason why the Ring of Fire can't be mined in a way that adds to, rather than subtracts from, the fabric of the region while contributing to First Nations, provincial, and federal coffers. The *Canadian Oxford Dictionary* defines the verb "share" as to "use or benefit from jointly with others." Let's get the definition right this time around.

What I envision is a model of mining that leverages traditional Indigenous knowledge and practice to ensure the land reverts to its natural state with no long-term environmental consequences once metals have been removed and shipped; that gives Indigenous peoples ownership of resources to be managed in a way that places people, flora, and fauna above profit on the priority list; and that balances economic prosperity with social and environmental posterity.

Some will regard my vision as overly optimistic and naïve. But if we are going to continue to embrace capitalism — and there is no real sign of the economic system waning — then at least let's introduce some fairness into the game. To carry on blindly in the pursuit of private profit, to reward greed, has been exposed as a sure-fire way to hasten the demise of the planet and the human race. In this age of frightening climate crisis, that approach is no longer feasible. In the words of Twiggy Forrest, the Wyloo controller who accumulated his immense wealth on the back of accelerating carbon emissions and who holds some sway over the fate of the James Bay Lowlands: "The party's over."

Leaders in government and the resource sector can do much better, starting with the Ring of Fire. They owe it to the seven generations to follow.

ACKNOWLEDGEMENTS

I owe deep gratitude to Neil Novak, whose enthusiasm and fine memory gave this book momentum despite my own reservations about tackling such a complex topic. Sadly, Noront founder Richard Nemis died six months before I started my research, but his sister Melody Nemis Henry helped sketch out the details of his childhood and early adult years.

Other Noront folks who helped me set the corporate history and regional geology straight include Alan Coutts, Matt Downey, and Ryan Weston. Meegwetch to Scott Jacob for sitting down with me at PDAC 2020 and introducing me to some of the other First Nations leaders involved in the Ring of Fire.

Thank you to the Ontario Arts Council for financial support during the research and writing stage. And to Stan Sudol for loaning me four banker's boxes of his own research on the topic.

I attribute the flow of the book to ECW editors Crissy Calhoun and David Marsh. They changed the text for the better in ways that would never have occurred to me. Thanks also go to co-publisher Jack David for taking a chance on a new author and to Sammy Chin for deftly managing so many moving parts in the creative process.

Cindy Andrew and Kathleen Coulson deserve a shout-out for accompanying me on a challenging canoe trip in the wild, bug-infested James Bay Lowlands and suffering through the resulting chapter; likewise James Hodgins for agreeing to be my poster boy for Sudbury economic diversification.

My MFA mentors at the University of King's College, Ken McGoogan and Lorri Neilsen Glenn, provided encouragement mixed with just the right pinch of criticism. Thanks also to the King's faculty and administrators, especially Stephen Kimber and Kim Pittaway, for concocting your special sauce of guidance, organization, and kindness during a challenging personal time. This book would never have come to fruition without you.

Some generous readers included Jeanne DesBrisay, Wendy Elliot, Charlotte Gray, Helen Heffernan, Teresa Heffernan, Cathy Matthews, Roger Moss, Christopher Murphy, Nancy Olivieri, Robin Pacific, and Dylan Reid. When I almost hung up my proverbial skates during the isolation of the COVID lockdown, my teammates from the Bill Bolton hockey league — too numerous to mention, but you know who you are — insisted I persevere. Thanks also go to Kate Chapman, Jeffron de Savoye, David Grierson, Missy Morlock, and Laurie Wilcox, and all six of my dear remaining Heffernan siblings, for unfailingly cheering me on from the stands.

KEY PLAYERS

Noront Resources

Alan Coutts, president and CEO (2013–2022)
Howard Lahti, former project geologist
John Harvey, former COO
Matt Downey, manager of lands and data
Neil Novak, VP of exploration (2003–2009)
Paul Semple, former COO (2009–2015)
Richard "Dick" Nemis, president and CEO (1983–2008)
Ryan Weston, VP of exploration (2016–2022)
Scott Jacob, manager of community relations (2010–2022)

Financiers

Andrew "Twiggy" Forrest, owner of Wyloo Metals Pty
Bill White, founder and chairman, IBK Capital
Robert Cudney, founder and CEO, Northfield Capital

First Nations

Brandyn Chum of Moose Cree Nation, and Noront employee
Bruce Achneepineskum, chief of Marten Falls
Chad Norman Day, president of Tahltan Central Government
Chris Moonias, former chief of Neskantaga
Elias Moonias, former chief of Marten Falls
James and Monique Kataquapit, Cree residents of Attawapiskat

Jerry Asp, former chief of Tahltan Nation

Matthew Coon Come, former national chief of the Assembly of First Nations

Scott Jacob, former chief of Webequie

Theresa Spence, former chief of Attawapiskat

Cliffs Natural Resources

David Anthony, former VP and senior project director

Richard Fink, former VP of ferroalloy operations

Freewest Resources

Don Hoy, VP of exploration

Mac Watson, president and CEO

KWG Resources

Frank Smeenk, president and CEO

Moe Lavigne, VP exploration and development

Tony Marquis, president of Canada Chrome, a KWG subsidiary

Spider Resources

Don MacFayden, geophysical consultant

Neil Novak, president and CEO

Public Servants

Dalton McGuinty, Ontario premier (2003–2013)

Doug Ford, Ontario premier (2018–)

Kathleen Wynne, Ontario premier (2013–2018)

Michael Gravelle, Ontario minister of Northern Development and Mines (2007–2011)

Other

Bob Rae, chief Ring of Fire negotiator for Matawa Tribal Council; former Ontario premier (1990–1995); 25th Canadian ambassador to the United Nations

Dayna Scott, associate professor, York Research Chair in Environmental Law and Justice

Frank Iacobucci, chief Ring of Fire negotiator for Ontario; retired Supreme Court justice

James Hodgins, Sudbury photographer

TIMELINE

1987	De Beers discovers kimberlite boulders in Attawapiskat River
1994	Spider-KWG joint venture (JV) discovers in situ kimberlites
2001	De Beers partners with Spider and KWG to form a JV
2002	Looking for diamond-bearing kimberlite, three-way JV intersects copper & zinc
2003	Dalton McGuinty elected premier
2006	Spider-KWG JV intersects chromite on Freewest's claims
2007	Noront discovers Ring of Fire nickel-copper deposit (Eagle's Nest)
2008	De Beers opens Victor diamond Mine
2008–9	Freewest discovers Black Thor and Black Label chromite deposits
2010	Cliffs purchases Freewest for C$240 million
	First Nations blockade Koper Lake and McFaulds Lake airstrips
	Cliffs acquires Spider for C$125 million
2012	Cliffs announces C$3.3 billion investment in Ring of Fire
2013	Cliffs abandons Canadian assets, including Ring of Fire
	Kathleen Wynne replaces McGuinty as premier
	Bob Rae and Frank Iacobucci appointed Ring of Fire negotiators
2014	Wynne announces C$1 billion road to Ring of Fire
2015	Noront buys Cliffs' Ring of Fire assets for C$20 million
2018	Doug Ford elected premier
	Rae and Iacobucci resign as negotiators

2020	Webequie and Marten Falls First Nations sign road agreement with Ontario
	Canada launches regional assessment for Ring of Fire
2021	Wyloo takes minority stake in Noront
	BHP and Wyloo engage in bidding war for Noront
2022	Wyloo acquires Noront for C$617 million
	Doug Ford reelected premier; appoints mines minister with Ring of Fire development mandate

NOTES

Introduction: Tremors of Disruption

1. Mike Ebbeling, "Neskantaga Stands Firmly in the Path of the Road," *CKDR News*, March 3, 2020.

Chapter I: Volcanoes, Glaciers, and Ancient Seas

1. Ryan Weston, "The Ring of Fire: Canada's Next Base Metal Mining Camp," YouTube video, March 3, 2021.
2. Dumont Nickel, "Dumont Nickel Project Overview," February 2021, https://dumontnickel.com/wp-content/uploads/2021/02/Dumont-Nickel-Project-Overview.pdf.
3. M.G. Houlé, C.M. Lesher, R.T. Metsaranta, A.A. Sappin, H.J.E. Carson, E.M. Schetselaar, V. McNicoll, and A. Laudadio, "Magmatic Architecture of the Esker Intrusive Complex in the Ring of Fire Intrusive Suite, McFaulds Lake Greenstone Belt, Superior Province, Ontario: Implications for the Genesis of Cr and Ni-Cu-(PGE) Mineralization in an Inflationary Dike-Chonolith-Sill Complex," Natural Resources Canada, 2020.
4. Jennifer La Grassa, "Electric Vehicle Battery Plant Set for Windsor, Ont., Signals Canada Is a 'Player' in Auto Industry's Future," *CBC News*, March 24, 2022.
5. James Mungall, "Stalled Ring of Fire Worth More Than $117 Billion," *Sudbury Star*, January 24, 2020.

Chapter 2: A Discovery in the Making

The discovery scenes and background are based almost entirely on personal communication with Richard Nemis's family, friends, and colleagues, including (in order of appearance) Neil Novak, Robert Cudney, David Graham, Elaine Finley, Melody Nemis Henry, John Harvey, Jennifer Nemis, Ryan Weston, and Bill White, as well as my own experience as a former staff writer for the *Northern Miner*. Press releases were helpful in piecing together the timeline.

1. Haida Nation v. British Columbia (Minister of Forests), 2004 SCC 73 (CanLII), 3 SCR 511.
2. Peter Koven, "So Much Cash on Hand, So Little on Hand to Buy," *National Post*, November 3, 2007.
3. Peter Koven, "Is This Voisey's Bay II? Nickel, Copper Grades at Noront's James Bay Double Eagle Project Are 'Unbelievable,'" *National Post*, October 13, 2007.
4. Cameron French, "Miners Rush to High-grade Nickel Strike," *Reuters*, October 17, 2007.
5. Jamie Sturgeon, "Noront Bows to Pressure from Dissident," *National Post*, October 28, 2008.

Chapter 3: Happy Accidents

Interviews with Neil Novak, Frank Smeenk, and Mackenzie Watson were used to construct developments from the early diamond exploration in the James Bay Lowlands to the discovery of the Ring of Fire nickel and chromium deposits. Personal accounts were checked against press releases and *The Geophysical History of Discoveries in the James Bay Lowlands from the Victor Kimberlite to the Ring of Fire Copper and Nickel Deposits* by R.L.S. Hogg and S. Munro in Proceedings of Exploration 17.

1. De Beers Group website, "Our Canada Story: History."
2. Sean Silcoff, "Bre-X's Sister Company Still Holds $27-Million in Cash," *National Post*, December 21, 2001.

3. Kim Hanson, "Two Bids Made for Saxton's Cuban Unit: Investment Firm Is Alleged to Have Misappropriated Money," *Financial Post*, February 1, 1999.
4. "OSC Approves Settlement for MacDonald Oil Exploration Ltd., MacDonald Mines Exploration Ltd., Mario Miranda and Frank Smeenk," Canada Newswire, January 12, 2001.
5. "MacDonald Mines JV with Falconbridge Not Proceeding," Canada Stockwatch, December 7, 2001.

Chapter 4: Cliffs Comes Calling

Former Cliffs managers David Anthony and Richard Fink provided input from Cliffs' perspective. Others weighed in on background, but not for attribution. Press releases issued by the American miner, KWG, and Freewest Resources as well as media reports from the time were helpful for confirmation. Encyclopedia Britannica's entry on chromium and Roskill's *Chromium Outlook to 2031*, 17th edition, were handy references.

1. N. Koleli and A. Demir, "Chromite," *Environmental Materials and Waste*, 2016.

Chapter 5: The Little Junior That Could

The corporate history of Noront Resources was gleaned from press releases and interviews with Noront managers Alan Coutts and Matt Downey and IBK Capital founder Bill White. Additional references include:

1. CMJ Staff, "Osisko Releases PEA on 'Highly Profitable' Gold Mine at Windfall in Quebec," *Canadian Mining Journal*, April 7, 2001.
2. Ryan Weston, "The Ring of Fire: Canada's Next Base Metal Mining Camp," YouTube video, March 3, 2021.
3. "Round Two for Richard Nemis," *Sudbury Mining Solutions Journal*, August 31, 2011.

4. "Round Two for Richard Nemis," *Sudbury Mining Solutions Journal*, August 31, 2011.

5. Shawn Bell, "Noront Wants to Be 'World-Class' in First Nations–Industry Relations," *Wataway News*, April 26, 2012.

6. Ian Ross, "Ring of Fire Developer Faces Tide of Opposition to Sault Ferrochrome Plant," *Northern Ontario Business*, October 17, 2019.

7. "Flow-Through Shares & the Mineral Exploration Tax Credit Explained," Prospectors & Developers Association of Canada, 2022, https://www.pdac.ca/priorities/access-to-capital/flow-through-shares.

8. Joy Liu, "BHP Billiton: Battery Industry's Demand for Nickel Expected to Surge by 1.3 Million Tons in Next Decade," *Steel News (Yieh Corp)*, January 4, 2022.

9. James Thomson, "Forrest Hails Fortescue Joint Venture with Indigenous Group," *Financial Review*, September 17, 2021.

10. Andrew Forrest, personal letter to Matawa Chiefs Council, June 1, 2021.

11. James Thomson, "Forrest Tops BHP Bid in Fight for Canadian Nickel Hopeful Noront," *Australian Financial Review*, December 13, 2021.

12. James Thomson, "Forrest Tops BHP Bid in Fight for Canadian Nickel Hopeful Noront," *Australian Financial Review*, December 13, 2021.

Chapter 6: Whose Land? Our Land

1. Roger Duhamel, *The James Bay Treaty: Treaty No. 9 (Made in 1905 and 1906) and Adhesions Made in 1929 and 1930*, reprinted from the edition of 1931 by © F.R.S.C. Queen's Printer and Controller of Stationery, Ottawa.

2. John Long, *Treaty No. 9: Making the Agreement to Share the Land in Far Northern Ontario in 1905* (Montreal and Kingston: McGill-Queen's University Press, 2010).

3. Ryan Moore, "This Is What Access to Clean Water Looks Like for a First Nation in a Remote Corner of Ontario," *Toronto Star*, April 17, 2020.

4. "Attawapiskat First Nation Declares State of Emergency after Suicide Attempts," *CTV News*, April 10, 2016.

5. "Indian Act," Canadian Encyclopedia, last modified February 7, 2006, https://www.thecanadianencyclopedia.ca/en/article/indian-act.

6. Bob Joseph, with Cynthia F. Joseph, *Indigenous Relations: Insights, Tips & Suggestions to Make Reconciliation a Reality* (Indigenous Relations Press/Page Two Books, 2019).

7. Bruce Cheadle and Stephanie Levitz, "Chief Counters Release of Audit with Explicit Demands from Feds for Change," Canadian Press, January 7, 2013.

8. Donna S. Martsolf and Claire Burke Draucker, "The Legacy of Childhood Sexual Abuse and Family Adversity," *Journal of Nursing Scholarship*, November 25, 2008, https://www.ncbi.nlm.nih.gov/pmc/articles/PMC3152829.

9. Nettie Wild, *Koneline: Our Land Beautiful*, film documentary, Canada Wild Productions, 2016.

10. Katie Hyslop, "Wet'suwet'en Crisis: Whose Rule of Law?," *Tyee*, February 14, 2020.

11. Personal communication, May 9, 2022.

12. Jeremiah Rodriguez, "Indigenous Population in Canada Could Climb to Nearly 3.2 million by 2041: StatCan," *CTV News*, October 6, 2021.

13. John Ivison, "With Millions Pouring into Attawapiskat, Colonial Blame Only Goes So Far," *National Post*, December 6, 2011.

14. Daniel Schwartz, "Deloitte's Audit of Northern Ontario First Nation Is Not the First to Raise Questions About Finances," *CBC News*, January 9, 2013.

15. Ron Grech, "Judge Calls Blockade an Act of Extortion," *Sudbury Star*, February 22, 2013, https://www.thesudburystar.com/2013/02/22/judge-calls-blockade-an-act-of-extortion.

16. "New Report Highlights the Essential Nature of Canadian Mining in Ongoing Global COVID-19 Economic Recovery Efforts," Mining Association of Canada, February 25, 2021.

17. J.P. Gladu, "Using Indigenous Peoples as Political Pawns in

Resource Development Is Simply Wrong," *Globe and Mail*, December 8, 2021.

Chapter 7: For Peat's Sake

1. Alison De Greef, *The Navachab Chronicles*, November 13, 1986.
2. J.L. Riley, *Wetlands of the Ontario Hudson Bay Lowland: A Regional Overview* (Toronto: Nature Conservancy of Canada, 2010), p. 156.
3. "Wetlands Hydrology Research Laboratory: James Bay Lowland," University of Waterloo, accessed April 28, 2022, https://uwaterloo .ca/wetlands-hydrology/research/james-bay-lowland-ontario -canada.
4. Canadian Oxford Dictionary, 1998.
5. "Northern Peatlands in Canada, an Enormous Carbon Storehouse," Wildlife Conservation Society Canada, 2021, accessed April 28, 2022, https://storymaps.arcgis.com/stories /19d24f59487b46f6a011dba140eddbe7.
6. Canadian Oxford Dictionary, 1998.
7. Michael A. Blaakman, "Dismal Swamp Company," MountVernon.org Digital Encyclopedia of George Washington, accessed April 28, 2022, https://www.mountvernon.org/library/digitalhistory/digital -encyclopedia/article/dismal-swamp-company.
8. Jessa Gamble, "What's at Stake in Ontario's Ring of Fire," *Canadian Geographic*, August 24, 2017.
9. "Mount Polley Mine Tailing Dam Breach," Government of British Columbia, accessed April 28, 2022, https://www2.gov.bc.ca /gov/content/environment/air-land-water/spills-environmental -emergencies/spill-incidents/past-spill-incidents/mt-polley.
10. "Independent Expert Engineering Investigation and Review Mount Polley Tailings Storage Facility Breach," Mount Polley Independent Expert Engineering Investigation and Review Panel, 2015, https://www.mountpolleyreviewpanel.ca/final-report.
11. Damien Cave, "Can a Carbon-Emitting Iron Ore Tycoon Save the Planet?," *New York Times*, October 16, 2021.
12. U. Rentel and M. Rentel, "Determining the Rehabilitation Success

of the Old Tailings Storage Facility of Navachab Gold Mine, Karibib, Namibia," in *Proceedings of the Fourth International Conference on Mine Closure*, edited by A.B. Fourie and M. Tibbett (Perth: Australian Centre for Geomechanics, 2009), pp. 109–121.

Chapter 8: Sudbury 2.0

1. A.J. Naldrett, "Evolution of Ideas About the Origin of the Sudbury Igneous Complex and Its Associated Ni-Cu-PGE Mineralization," in *Ontario Geological Survey Open File Report 6243: A Field Guide to the Geology of Sudbury, Ontario*, edited by Don H. Rousell and G. Heather Brown (Sudbury: Ontario Geological Survey, 2009).

2. Michael Marshall, "Timeline: The Evolution of Life," *New Scientist*, July 14, 2009.

3. Edward S. Rogers and Donald B. Smith, *Aboriginal Ontario: Historical Perspectives on the First Nations* (Toronto: Dundurn Press, 1994).

4. O.W. Saarinen, "Sudbury," Canadian Encyclopedia, last modified October 21, 2012, https://thecanadianencyclopedia.ca/en/article/sudbury-greater.

5. James Morrison, *The Robinson Treaties of 1850: A Case Study Prepared for the Royal Commission on Aboriginal Peoples* (Ottawa: Government of Canada Publications, 1996).

6. James Hopkin, "Court Rules in Favour of Robinson Huron Treaty Beneficiaries," *Soo Today*, June 28, 2020.

7. Tom Jewiss, "The Mining History of the Sudbury Area," from *Rocks and Minerals in Canada* (Waterloo: University of Waterloo, 1983).

8. A. Murray, "Report for the Year 1856" in *Geological Survey of Canada, Report of Activities, 1853–1856*, pp. 180–181 (Ottawa: Geological Survey of Canada, 1857).

9. J.P. Golightly, "The Ni-Cu-PGE Deposits of the Sudbury Igneous Complex," in *Ontario Geological Survey Open File Report 6243: A Field Guide to the Geology of Sudbury, Ontario*, edited by Don

H. Rousell & G. Heather Brown (Sudbury: Ontario Geological Survey, 2009), chapter 12.

10. John Gunn, "'Moonscape' Sudbury Deserves Global Recognition for Its Environmental 180," *Sudbury.com*, June 6, 2019.

11. David Lewis Stein, "Sudbury: The City That Lost a War between Unions," *Maclean's*, April 2, 1962.

12. Darren MacDonald, "One Day Longer, Ten Years Later," *Sudbury.com*, 2009, https://www.sudbury.com/vale-strike.

13. "Inco's Miners Irked by Layoffs," *New York Times*, February 19, 1972.

14. Tristin Hopper, "A B.C. Museum Says It's Preserved the Railcar from Which Pierre Trudeau Gave the Finger To Protesters," Postmedia Breaking News, August 22, 2016.

15. Tony Van Alphen, "In Sudbury It's Restive, Not Festive," *Toronto Star*, December 19, 2009.

16. Philip Shabecoff, "Ontario Announces Program to Sharply Curtail Acid Rain," *New York Times*, December 18, 1985.

17. Livio Di Matteo, "The Long Saga of Arrested Development in Northern Ontario," *Timmins Today*, July 17, 2021.

Chapter 9: A Tale of Two Provinces

1. Magnus Isacsson, *Power*, film documentary, National Film Board of Canada, 1996.

2. Sam Howe Verhovek, "Cuomo, Citing Economic Issues, Cancels Quebec Power Contract," *New York Times*, March 28, 1992.

3. Bill Gallagher, *Resource Rulers: Fortune and Folly on Canada's Road to Resources* (Waterloo: Bill J.W. Gallagher, 2012).

4. "Natives Protest Labrador Megaplan; Newfoundland, Quebec Launch Talks on 2nd Hydro Project," *Toronto Star*, March 10, 1998.

5. Graeme Hamilton, "Why Quebec's Cree Are Thriving While Misery Reigns across James Bay at Attawapiskat," *National Post*, April 15, 2016.

Chapter 10: From Backrooms to Bulldozers

1. Patrick Brown, *Mountie in Mukluks: The Arctic Adventures of Bill White* (Pender Harbour: Harbour Publishing, 2004).
2. Tim Edwards, "Bill White: Trapper Sailor Fighter Cop," *Uphere*, September 14, 2018.
3. "NW Ont. First Nation Plans Blockade of Exploration Activity in Ring of Fire Area," Canadian Press, January 18, 2010.
4. Tanya Talaga, "This Frozen Patch of Earth," *Toronto Star*, March 27, 2010.
5. Rick Garrick, "Ambitious Timeline for Ring of Fire," *Wataway News*, July 7, 2011.
6. Michael Gravelle, "A Letter to the Honourable Greg Rickford, Federal Minister of Natural Resources," December 11, 2014.
7. Section 35, Constitution Act, 1982.
8. Jody Porter, "Kathleen Wynne to First Nations Chiefs: Do Not 'Squander' $1B Ring of Fire Promise," *CBC News*, May 12, 2017.
9. Wayne Moonias, "A Letter to Premier Kathleen Wynne Re: Ring of Fire Extinguishment of Our Rightful Claims," February 22, 2017.
10. Jorge Barrera, "Ontario Playing Favourites with First Nations on Ring of Fire, Say Chiefs," *CBC News*, November 23, 2018.
11. Matt Prokopchuk, "Ontario Government Ends Ring of Fire Regional Agreement with Matawa First Nations," *CBC News*, August 27, 2018.
12. Gloria Galloway, "Court Cancels Mining Permit after Ontario Failed to Adequately Consult First Nation Community," *Globe and Mail*, July 17, 2018.

Chapter 11: Circus Acts

1. *Science for a Changing Far North* in The Report of the Far North Science Advisory Panel, 2010.
2. "EC Advice to CEAA, Ontario Region, Regarding Cliff's Chromite Mine," Environment Canada, September 12, 2011.

3. Jody Porter, "Northern Ontario's Ring of Fire a Hot Election Issue," *CBC News*, September 9, 2011.

4. Dariya Baiguzhiyeva, "First Nations Chiefs Concerned with Ring of Fire Process," *TBnewswatch.com*, January 24, 2022.

5. "NAN Endorses Plan to Repeal Far North Act," *Timmins Daily Press*, February 27, 2019.

6. Dayna Scott and John Cutfeet, "After the Far North Act: Indigenous Jurisdiction in Ontario's Far North," *Yellowhead Institute*, July 9, 2019.

7. Stan Sudol, "Accent: A Slow Road to the Ring," *Sudbury Star*, June 3, 2018.

8. "Ottawa's Ring of Fire Assessment Process Declared Unconstitutional by Alberta Court," *Timmins Today*, May 17, 2022.

9. Heather Exner-Pirot, "The Trudeau Government Can No Longer 'Freeze Out' Pro-Development First Nations," *Natchaptional Post*, August 11, 2021.

10. "NAN Chiefs Oppose Ontario Omnibus Bill 132," *Sudbury.com*, November 15, 2019.

11. "Collaborating with Far North First Nations to Promote Economic Growth and Job Creation," Northern Development, Mines, Natural Resources and Forestry Ontario, November 9, 2021.

12. Alisha Hiyate, "Progress or Peril? First Nations in the Ring of Fire Divided on Infrastructure — and the Mining Development It Would Attract," *Canadian Mining Journal*, March 19, 2022.

Chapter 12: Planes, Trains, or Automobiles?

1. *Ice Road Truckers*, Season 1, Episode 1: "Ready to Roll," 2007.

2. "Tractor 'Trains' Move Freight in Far North," *Popular Mechanics*, January, 1935.

3. Marcus Gee, "The Thin White Line: How Northern Ontario's Winter Roads Are Built," *Globe and Mail*, February 23, 2020.

4. Ekati Diamond Mine and Diavik Diamond Mine Winter

Road Joint Venture, accessed 2022, https://jvtcwinterroad.ca/construction.

5. Leah Meirovich, "Canada's Ice Road Opens for Milestone Year," *Rapaport's Diamonds.net*, February 7, 2019.

6. Karen Mazurkewich, "Romancing the Stone," *Financial Post*, November 3, 2007.

7. *Canada's Changing Climate Report*, Environment and Climate Change Canada, April 2, 2019.

8. Crystal Gail Fraser, "The New Road in the North," *The Walrus*, November 27, 2019.

9. Stan Sudol, "KWG — the Chromite Mouse That Roars," *Sudbury Star*, November 14, 2013.

10. "Apology for Aboriginal Burial Ground Blunder Not Enough, Says Marten Falls Chief," Canadian Press, April 14, 2020.

11. Sarath Vala and Deepak Manglorkar, *Canada Chrome Corporation Rail vs. Road Trade-off Study*, Tetra Tech, February 9, 2013.

12. "Premier Doug Ford's Hopes for Ontario's Electric Vehicle Industry Hinge on Mining Its Ring of Fire," *Miningconnection.com*, November 9, 2021.

13. Webequie Supply Road Project, Ref # 80183, Wildlands League, January 27, 2020.

14. Jim Moodie, "KWG Forging Ahead with Ring of Fire Railroad: Capreol Native Tapped to Oversee $2B Infrastructure Project," *Sudbury Star*, February 7, 2021.

Conclusion: Keep the Faith

1. Jonathan Berger and Thomas Terry, *Canoe Atlas of the Little North* (Ontario: Boston Mills Press, 2007).

2. J.L. Riley, *Wetlands of the Ontario Hudson Bay Lowland: A Regional Overview* (Toronto: Nature Conservancy of Canada, 2011), p. 156.

3. Far North Science Advisory Panel (Ont.), "Science for a Changing Far North: The Report of the Far North Science Advisory Panel, April 2010" (Ontario: Queen's Printer for Ontario, 2010).

4. Elyn R. Humphreys, Chris Charron, Mathew Brown, and Randall Jones, "Two Bogs in the Canadian Hudson Bay Lowlands and a Temperate Bog Reveal Similar Annual Net Ecosystem Exchange of CO_2," *Arctic, Antarctic, and Alpine Research*, Vol. 46, No. 1, 2014, pp. 103–113.

5. William A. Niering and Nancy C. Olmstead, *The Audubon Society Field Guide to North American Wildflowers, Eastern Region* (New York: Knopf, 1979), p. 752.

INDEX

Ring of Fire, 11, 48, 50, 54, 61–62; end of project, 59; and Noront, 62; sills deposit in Ring of Fire, 17; transportation, 155, 156, 157

chromium: as commodity, 48, 53–54; deposits in Ring of Fire, 17, 20

Chum, Brandyn, 83

Churchill Falls (Labrador) power dam, 125–26

claims (mineral or mining claims): on esker, 57, 155–56; law in Ontario, 7–8; online system, 143; process and registration, 8; in Ring of Fire, 33; for transportation, 56

Clement, Tony, 135

Cliffs Natural Resources: assets purchased, 67; and chromite, 54–56; jump into Ring of Fire, 53, 59, 131; and negotiations, 133, 134; pullout of Ring of Fire, 59, 134, 140; setbacks in Canada, 58–59; takeover of Freewest, 55; transportation to/from Ring of Fire, 57–58, 134–35, 156

climate change, 99, 101, 151

Coastal GasLink pipeline, 88

Cobalt (Ontario) mines, 142

comet and crater near Sudbury, 106–7, 108

Connors, Stompin' Tom, 113

Constitution Act (1982), 8, 135

consultation of Indigenous peoples: and anti-development assumption, 144–45; changes and reduction in Ontario, 145–46, 153; as constitutional right, 8, 173; for De Beers/Victor mine, 90; description, 8, 143; establishment as legal precedent, 25; and IBAs, 117; Kitchenuhmaykoosib Inninuwug (KI) case, 130–31, 141; in La Grande development, 123; Landore Resources Canada case, 138; by Ontario government, 130–34, 137, 145–46, 153; in Ontario Mining Act, 8, 130, 143; and Ring of Fire, 9, 131–32

Coon Come, Matthew, 121, 122, 124

copper, 20

copper-zinc, in Ring of Fire, 68

copper-zinc deposits, creation, 17–18

Córrego do Feijão dam failure (Brazil), 102

Coutts, Alan, 66–67, 71, 72–73

Cree (in Ontario): in Ring of Fire area, 8, 78; support for, 127

Cree (in Quebec): agreement with Quebec, 126–27; consultation, 123;

ferrochrome smelter in Sault Ste. Marie, 68–69

Fiddler, Alvin, 79, 143–44, 145

Fink, Richard, 54, 59, 144

Finley, Elaine, 30

First Nations: care for the land, 77; in challenges of project, 9; community need and wants, 57; consultation (*See* consultation of Indigenous peoples); decision-making, 78, 89; environmental assessments for road, 70; families as leaders, 89; and Far North Act (FNA), 143–45; and future of Ring of Fire, 173; in imagined future of Ring of Fire, 166, 167, 170–71, 173, 174; impact of settlers and roads, 7, 10, 160; infrastructure before development, 11–12; land use plans, 144; legal wins, 173; letter from Forrest, 72; moratorium on development in Ring of Fire, 92–93; one-on-one agreements with Ontario, 137–38, 146; opposition to Noront development, 70–71, 79–81; regional environmental assessments, 139–40, 141; relations with Noront, 64–65, 67, 70–71, 74; role in projects, 93; support for Ring of Fire, 83, 92; water and boil-water advisory, 79, 80; in Yehewin Aski, 77–78. *See also* Indigenous peoples and communities; *specific communities and nations*

Five Nations Energy Inc. (FNEI), 160

flow-through financing, 70

Ford, Doug: approach to First Nations, 136, 137–38, 146, 153; Far North development, 145; as premier, 136, 159; proposed road to Ring of Fire, 11, 137–38, 153, 158–59

Forrest, Andrew "Twiggy," 71, 72, 73, 74, 103

Fortescue Metals Group, 71, 72, 103

Fox, Derek, 146

Franco-Nevada, 67, 70

Franklin, Jim, 140

Fraser, Crystal Gail, 151

Fraser, Horace, 22

"free, prior, and informed consent" as potential veto, 8

Freewest Resources: base metal discovery, 45, 46, 48; chromite, 11, 50, 54–55; takeover by Noront, 55

Gallagher, Bill, 125

infrastructure: lack for First Nations, 80; to Moosonee and west to Ring of Fire, 159–60; need for, 11–12; in northern Quebec, 154; pledges by governments, 2; power and internet to Ring of Fire, 118

Innu people, 126

Inuit: consultation in Quebec, 123; impact of gold mining, 84–85; Odeyak protest journey, 121–22; writings on, 129. *See also* Indigenous peoples

investment and investors in Ring of Fire: cyclical market for financing, 44; interest in, 33–34; promotion of, 28–29, 30

iron ore, 58

Irwin, Warren, 34, 35–36

Jacob, Scott, 5, 6–7, 10, 11, 25–26

James Bay and Northern Quebec Agreement, 123–24, 125

James Bay Treaty. *See* Treaty 9

Jennifer (daughter of R. Nemis), 32, 69–70

Jericho diamond mine, 150–51

Joseph, Bob, 81

Joudrey, James, 114

junior mining companies, description and role, 29, 52–53

Juno Corp., 68

Kabenung Lake cabins of Nemis, 32–33

Kamerman, Linda, 156

Kataquapit, James, 76–77

Kent, Peter, 139

Kiiwetinoong riding, 160

kimberlite, 38–40, 41–42, 43

Kitchenuhmaykoosib Inninuwug (KI) First Nation, 130–31, 141

Kivalliq Inuit Association (KIA), 84

Koneline: Our Land Beautiful (movie), 85, 86, 87

Kuczma, Anastasia Maria (aka "Chrissie"), 31

KWG Resources: chromite, 54, 56; diamonds exploration, 40, 42; joint venture with De Beers, 43–44; railroad to Ring of Fire, 155–56, 160–61; transportation to/from Ring of Fire, 57–58. *See also* Spider-KWG

Noront Resources (2008–2022, post–Richard Nemis era): approval of Eagle's Nest and Blackbird, 67–68; exploration and drilling in Ring of Fire, 64; ferrochrome smelter in Sault Ste. Marie, 68–69; financing and acquisition, 70, 71–74; gold and chromite in Ring of Fire, 62, 68; investment in, 64; management and board, 62, 67; opposition from First Nations, 70–71, 79–81; relations with First Nations, 64–65, 67, 70–71, 74; shares and shareholding, 65, 70, 71, 73–74; tailings and water in Ring of Fire, 103; takeover of Freewest, 55; VMS discovery, 68

Noront Steel, 31, 60, 112

the North, warming trend in, 151

The Northern Miner, description and work at, 29–30

Northern Road Link. *See* proposed road to Ring of Fire

Northwest Territories (NWT): diamonds discoveries, 42, 150; winter roads, 147–48, 149–51

NOT-07-01 drill hole, 22, 23

Novak, Neil: base metal discovery in Ring of Fire, 45–46, 48; Bill Dennis Award, 50; core sample from Ring of Fire, 21–22; description and background, 22–23; diamond exploration, 40–43; in discovery story, 22, 23, 25, 26; interview with, 21; takeover of Spider by Cliffs, 56

Odeyak journey (protest), 121–22, 124

O'Donohoe, Deirdre, 43

Ojibway: life and settlers in Sudbury area, 109–10, 112; in Ring of Fire area, 8, 78; treaty, 110

Oji-Cree, in Ring of Fire area, 8, 78

Ontario: economic contribution of mining, 142–43; law for mineral claims, 7–8; ridings near Ring of Fire, 160; watersheds on James Bay, 162–63; white settlement in north, 7; winter roads, 153, 154

Ontario Court of Appeal, 130

Ontario Geological Survey, 43

Ontario government: agreement for road with First Nations, 136, 155, 158; approval of Eagle's Nest and Blackbird, 67; challenges of Ring of Fire project, 9; consultation with First Nations, 130–34, 137, 145–46, 153; critical-minerals strategy, 94; and future of Ring

Red Chris mine project, 87–88

red knot (bird), 98

regional environmental assessments for Ring of Fire, 92–93, 139–41, 159, 173–74

residential schools, 82–83

Resource Capital Funds, 64, 70, 71

resource development in Canada: *vs.* conservation, 86; constitutional right of Indigenous peoples, 8; support by Indigenous peoples, 144–45; sustainable development, 173; veto on, 8

resource development *vs.* nature, 97–98, 104

retail (non-professional) investor, 30

Richard Jr. (son of Nemis), 32

Richard Nemis Ring of Fire First Nations Community Trust, 69–70

Rickford, Greg, 11, 135

Riley, John, 100

Ring of Fire: challenges of project, 9; core sample description, 21–22; description, 2, 8; discovery, 22, 23–27; discovery announcements, 26, 27, 34; as ecosystem, 98–99, 169–70; employment in, 118–19; first nickel discovery, 6–7, 25; framework for development, 133; future of region, 172–75; geological creation, 14–15, 16–18, 21–22, 99, 169; as greenstone belt, 19, 99; imagined future, 166–68, 170–71, 173–75; Indigenous groups in area, 8, 78; infrastructure (*See* infrastructure); minerals found, 2, 8, 19, 116–17; minimal footprint in, 117; moratorium on development, 92–93; naming and name, 16, 27–28; as opportunity in Ontario, 132–33; potential for model of resource management, 9–10, 93, 94; potential impact, 76; regional environmental assessments, 92–93, 139–41, 159, 173–74; renewable energy in, 166; rocks formation, 15; as source for EV and renewable energy, 9, 10, 93–94; spill potential, 102–3; underground mines, 76, 103, 108. *See also specific topics, nations, or persons*

Ring of Fire, in Pacific Ocean, 16

"Ring of Fire" (song), 16, 28

Ring of Fire Secretariat, 132

Riopelle, Robert, 91

roads and road-building: access to Matawa communities now, 164; agreement of Ontario government with First Nations, 136, 155,